A BOOK AT BATHTIME

FRANK MUIR

HEINEMANN : LONDON

William Heinemann Ltd
10 Upper Grosvenor Street, London W1X 9PA
LONDON   MELBOURNE   TORONTO
JOHANNESBURG   AUCKLAND

First published 1982
© Frank Muir 1982

434 48153 X

Phototypeset by Tradespools Ltd, Frome
Somerset

Printed and bound in Great Britain by
Richard Clay (The Chaucer Press) Ltd, Bungay, Suffolk

A BOOK AT
BATHTIME

IN THE BATH

by Michael Flanders and Donald Swann

To be sung whilst taking a bath. Unaccompanied.

A percussion rhythm may be added with the aid of two toothbrushes and an empty glass.

Warmly flowing ♩ = 104

1. Oh, I find much sim-ple plea-sure when I've
2. Oh, my loa-thing for my fel-lows ri-ses

had a tir-ing day } In the bath, in the bath! { Where the
stea-ming from my brain } { And con-

noise of gen-tle spon-ging seems to blend with my top A, In the
-den-seth to the Milk of Hu-man Kind-ness once a-gain In the

bath, in the bath! To the
bath, la-la-la-la-la, in the bath! Oh, the

skirl of pipes vi-bra-ting in the boi-ler room be-low I
ting-ling of the scrub-bing brush, the flan-nel's soft ca-ress! To

sing a pot-pour-ri of all the songs I used to know, And the
wield a lord-ly loo-fah is a joy I can't ex-press. How

wa- ter thun- ders in and gur- gles
tru- ly it is spo- ken, one is

down the o- ver- flow } In the bath, in the bath!
next to God- li- ness

INTRODUCTION

A recent study of reading habits (*Book Industry Study Group Report No.* 6, 1978) revealed, without much pleasure, that as many readers do their reading in bathrooms as in libraries.

Many volumes have been written in the hope that they will be brooded upon in the dry silence of a library. In the light of the above statistic, it seemed high time that a modest volume was addressed specifically to the other half; to those who enjoy a read in the gurgling privacy of their bathroom.

It also seemed appropriate that as the impetus of this modest volume was the revelation that the bathroom is more than it seems in our social life, its subject should be an investigation into what part the bath, and the other facilities of a bathroom, played in the social life of our forefathers.

Letters, memoirs, poems, stories and gossip reveal that this social life was indeed 'social'. Only in comparatively recent years have we decided that we can only decently take a bath or perform our natural functions when we are alone. And only in even more recent years have we regularly smothered ourselves in lather, holding that Cleanliness is next to Godliness.

The concept of our modern bathroom as a hygienic, deodorized module with everything built-in is less than a hundred years old. As we glance round its constituent parts we can compare them with the facilities which our ancestors had to do battle with. How they coped is revealed in their writings. We learn of Disraeli, whose wife had to pull the string on his cold shower; of the Marquise who boiled her leg in the Seine; of Balzac whose ambition in life was to become so famous that he would be allowed to break wind in society;

1

of the lady in the public privy in Holland who kindly offered an English gentleman the loan of her mussel-shell scraper when she had finished with it. We also learn of the social dilemmas brought about by the W.C. (or whatever you call it) never having been given a simple, acceptable name, thus plunging posterity into the agony of having to sort out a mess of euphemisms; to separate, as it were, the U-bend words from the non-U-bend words.

For background information on the subject of bathrooms I am happily indebted to that Bible of Bathrooms, *Clean and Decent* by Lawrence Wright. Also to an odd volume of much charm and erudition, written it seems during the war whilst on Air Raid Precautions watch in Chelsea, *Cleanliness and Godliness*, by Reginald Reynolds.

> 'Go little book, on your chosen path
> To learning on the loo, laughter in the bath . . .'

Frank Muir
THORPE, 1982

P. S. Advances in modern science and technology have provided the solution to a problem which has bedevilled cleanly readers for centuries: how to read in a hot bath without your spectacles steaming up. You dip your spectacles into the hot bath for a moment and then polish them dry with a handy length of soft tissue.

There it rests, dominating the bathroom; a long rectangle of smooth porcelain falling into deep soft curves; unchanged in shape from the one into which King Midas of Knossos stepped some 3700 years ago.

Taking a bath is, to some people, a necessary chore to be got through as rapidly as possible, like cleaning one's shoes.

To a distinguished and immensely prolific modern author it was something else entirely:

> Lying in a hot bath, smoking a pipe. And Elagabalus himself, after driving his white horses through the gold-dusted streets of Rome, never knew anything better; nor indeed anything as good, not having either pipe or tobacco. People still say to me 'The way you work!', and behind the modest smirk I laugh secretly, knowing myself to be one of the laziest and most self-indulgent men alive. Long after they have caught the 8.20, opened the morning mail, telephoned to the managing director of the Cement Company, dictated yet another appeal to the Board of Trade, I am lying in my hot bath, smoking a pipe. I am not even soaping and scrubbing, but simply lying there, like a pink porpoise, puffing away. In a neighbouring room, thrown on the floor, are the morning papers, loud with more urgent demands for increased production, clamouring for every man and woman to save the country. And there I am,

lost in steam, the fumes of Latakia, and the vaguest dreams. Just beyond the bolted door, where the temperature drops nearly to freezing point, are delicate women, who have already been up for hours, toiling away. And do I care? Not a rap. Sometimes I pretend, just to test the credulity of the household, that I am planning my day's work; but I am doing nothing of the kind. Often I do not intend to do any work at all during the day; and even when I know I must do some, I could not possibly plan it, in or out of a bath. No, I am just lying there, a pampered slug, with my saurian little eyes half-closed, cancelling the Ice Ages, lolling again in the steamy hot morning of the world's time, wondering dimly what is happening to Sir Stafford Cripps. '. . . One of the most energetic and prolific of our authors. . . .' *Gertcha!*

J. B. Priestley (*1894–*)
DELIGHTS, 1949

Perhaps Mr. Priestley's pleasure was heightened by the knowledge that he was in no danger where he was:

'People born to be hanged are safe in water.'

Mark Twain's mother
Quoted in MARK TWAIN, A BIOGRAPHY, A. B. Paine

Young Master Robin, at prayers, remembered his romp in the bath with pleasure too:

God Bless Mummy. I know that's right.
Wasn't it fun in the bath to-night?
The cold's so cold, and the hot's so hot.
Oh! *God Bless Daddy* – I quite forgot.

A. A. Milne (*1882–1956*)
WHEN WE WERE VERY YOUNG

Getting up in the morning in the sixteenth century was rather different from today. A noted medical man of the time recommended it be accomplished with a light laugh and a prayer but not much in the way of ablutions:

> When you do rise in the morning, rise with mirth, and remember God. Let your hose be brushed within and without, and flavour the inside of them against the fire; use linen socks or linen hose next to your legs. When you be out of your bed, stretch forth your legs and your arms, and your body; cough and spit, and then go to your stool to make your egestion; and exonerate yourself at all times that nature would expel. After you have evacuated your body and trussed your points, comb your head oft; and so do divers times in the day. And wash your hands and wrists, your face and eyes, and your teeth, with cold water.

Andrew Boorde *(1490?–1549)*
DYETARY

When Lady Ruthven visited the young Pauline Borghese in Rome she found that personal cleanliness in 1862 among aristocrats was not vigorously pursued:

> When the guests arrived, they found the Princess – supremely lovely – with her beautiful little white feet exposed upon a velvet cushion. Then two or three maids came in, and touched the feet with a sponge and dusted them with a little powder – 'c'était la toilette des pieds.' The Duke of Hamilton used to take up one of the little feet and put it inside his waistcoat 'like a little bird'.

Augustus Hare *(1834–1903)*
THE STORY OF MY LIFE

The little Princess clearly did not have an English nanny to remind her of her obligations:

> 'We don't like that girl from Tooting Bec,
> She washes her face and forgets her neck.'
>
> Quoted in NANNY SAYS. (1972) Sir Hugh Casson and Joyce Grenfell

The Ancient Greeks and Romans had large and elaborate bath houses with water at varying temperatures. These became popular places to meet friends, cadge a free dinner, gossip. Slaves were on hand to anoint with oils, massage and generally mop up. But not everybody could be bothered with bathing. One mathematician, head full of isosceles triangles and acute angles, had to be forcibly cleansed:

> Oftimes his [Archimedes'] servants got him
> against his will to the baths, to wash and anoint
> him: and yet being there, he would ever be
> drawing out of the geometrical figures, even in the
> very imbers of the chimney. And while they were
> anointing of him with oils and sweet savours, with
> his fingers he did draw lines upon his naked body:
> so far was he taken from himself, and brought into
> an extasy or trance, with the delight he had in the
> study of geometry.
>
> Plutarch (*1st. century A.D.*)
> LIVES

The Ancients seemed to bath in considerable comfort. Even a Chinese Emperor's new concubine could count on a dip in a nice warm vase whilst on call:

> Two days, two nights, and she was still in the
> royal bed-chamber. Three times he slept and each
> time she went to the door and beckoned to her
> serving woman, and the woman came creeping
> through the curtains to the boudoir beyond. There

the eunuchs had prepared a ready bath, a cauldron of water upon coals, so that the woman needed only to dip the water into the vast porcelain jar and make her mistress fresh again. She had brought clean garments and different robes and she brushed Yehonala's hair and coiled it smoothly. Not once did the young girl speak except to give direction and not once did the serving woman ask a question. Each time when her task was done Yehonala went in again to the imperial bedroom and the heavy doors were closed behind the yellow curtains.

Pearl S. Buck (*1892–1973*)
IMPERIAL WOMEN

In Turkey the ancient tradition of communal hot baths was maintained with such national enthusiasm that these steamy affairs became known to Europeans as 'Turkish Baths'. The first Englishwoman to penetrate one of these was Lady Mary Wortley Montagu, who wrote to a friend:

I won't trouble you with a relation of our tedious journey; but I must not omit what I saw remarkable at Sophia, one of the most beautiful towns in the Turkish empire, and famous for its hot baths, that are resorted to both for diversion and health. I stopped here one day on purpose to see them. Designing to go *incognita*, I hired a Turkish coach. These voitures are not at all like ours, but much more convenient for the country, the heat being so great that glasses would be very troublesome. They are made a good deal in the manner of the Dutch coaches, having wooden lattices painted and gilded; the inside being painted with baskets and nosegays of flowers, intermixed commonly with little poetical mottoes. They are covered all over with scarlet cloth, lined with silk, and very often richly embroidered and fringed. This cover-

7

ing entirely hides the persons in them, but may be thrown back at pleasure, and the ladies peep through the lattices. They hold four people very conveniently, seated on cushions, but not raised.

In one of these covered wagons, I went to the bagnio about ten o'clock. It was already full of women. It is built of stone, in the shape of a dome, with no windows but in the roof, which gives light enough. There were five of these domes joined together, the outmost being less than the rest, and serving only as a hall, where the portress stood at the door. Ladies of quality generally give this woman the value of a crown or ten shillings; and I did not forget that ceremony. The next room is a very large one paved with marble, and all round it, raised, two sofas of marble, one above another. There were four fountains of cold water in this room, falling first into marble basins, and then running on the floor in little channels made for that purpose, which carried the streams into the next room, something less than this, with the same sort of marble sofas, but so hot with steams of sulphur proceeding from the baths joining to it, it was impossible to stay there with one's clothes on. The two other domes were the hot baths, one of which had cocks of cold water turning into it, to temper it to what degree of warmth the bathers have a mind to.

I was in my travelling habit, which is a riding dress, and certainly appeared very extraordinary to them. Yet there was not one of them that shewed the least surprise or impertinent curiosity, but received me with all the obliging civility possible. I know no European court where the ladies would have behaved themselves in so polite a manner to a stranger. I believe in the whole, there were two hundred women, and yet none of those disdainful smiles, or satiric whispers, that never fail in our assemblies when anybody appears that is not dressed exactly in the fashion. They repeated over and over to me, 'Uzelle, pék uzelle', which is nothing but Charming, very charming. The first sofas were covered with cushions and rich carpets, on which sat the ladies; and on the second, their slaves behind them, but without any distinction of rank by their dress, all being in the state of nature, that is, in plain English, stark naked, without any beauty or defect concealed. Yet there was not the least wanton smile or immodest gesture among them. They walked and moved with the same majestic grace which Milton describes of our general mother. There were many amongst them as exactly proportioned as ever any goddess was drawn by the pencil of Guido or Titian, – and most of their skins shiningly white, only adorned by their beautiful hair divided in many tresses, hanging on their shoulders, braided either with pearl or ribbon, perfectly representing the figures of the Graces.

I was here convinced of the truth of a reflection I had often made, that if it was the fashion to go naked, the face would be hardly observed. I perceived that the ladies with the finest skins and most delicate shapes had the greatest share of my admiration, though their faces were sometimes less beautiful than those of their companions. To tell you the truth, I had wickedness enough to wish secretly that Mr. Jervas could have been there invisible. I fancy it would have very much improved his art, to see so many fine women naked, in different postures, some in conversation, some working, others drinking coffee or sherbet, and many negligently lying on their cushions, while their slaves (generally pretty girls of seventeen or eighteen) were employed in braiding their hair in several pretty fancies. In short, it is the women's coffee-house, where all the news of the town is told, scandal invented, &c. – They generally take this diversion once a week, and stay there at least four or five hours, without getting cold by immediate coming out of the hot bath into the cold room, which was very surprising to me. The lady that seemed the most considerable among them, entreated me to sit by her, and would fain have undressed me for the bath. I excused myself with some difficulty. They being all so earnest in persuading me, I was at last forced to open my shirt, and shew them my stays; which satisfied them·very well, for, I saw, they believed I was so locked up in that machine, that it was not in my own power to open it, which contrivance they attributed to my husband.

Lady Mary Wortley Montagu (*1689–1762*)
Letter to the Lady Rich, Adrianople, 1 April, 1717.

In more recent times a literary gentleman from America tried the baths and emerged unimpressed:

Here endeth my experience of the celebrated
Turkish bath, and here also endeth my dream of
the bliss the mortal revels in who passes through it.
It is a malignant swindle. The man who enjoys it is
qualified to enjoy anything that is repulsive to sight
or sense . . .

Mark Twain (*1835–1910*)
THE INNOCENTS ABROAD

The sexes were usually segregated at these communal bath houses but a little mixed bathing was noticed by Pliny the Elder. According to first-hand reports from the poets Martial and Juvenal, ladies who dived in with the gentlemen were either whores or intellectuals (or both?). Mixed bathing was frowned upon but became prevalent in the Middle Ages when the baths were little more than brothels. Indeed the Italian word for bath *bagno*, and the English word *stews*, became synonyms for 'brothel'.

The nearest that the British got to the Roman/Turkish tradition of treating the bath house as the equivalent of a golf clubhouse or a W.I. Sewing Afternoon, or a house of assignation, was the development of Watering-Places, or Spas as they came to be called after the Belgian town of Spa where the whole thing started.

In 1606 it was discovered that a spring in the little town of Tunbridge, Kent, produced 'chalybeate waters' (chalybeate – not a word that drops from one's lips daily – means 'containing iron'). Citizens became convinced that if they forced some of this stuff down daily it would cure them of almost everything wrong with them so Tunbridge Wells – later Royal Tunbridge Wells – became a famous Watering-Place. A poet describes the elegant society to be met there in the seventeenth century:

At Five this Morn, when Phoebus rais'd his
   Head
From Thetis' Lap, I rais'd myself from Bed;
And mounting Steed, I trotted to the Waters,
The Rendezvous of Fools, Buffoons, and
   Praters,
Cuckolds, Whores, Citizens, their Wives and
   Daughters.
My squeamish Stomach I with Wine had
   brib'd,
To undertake the Dose that was prescrib'd;
But turning Head, a sudden cursed Crew
That innocent Provision overthrew,
Did, without drinking, make me purge and spew.

From Coach and Six a Thing unweildy roll'd,
Whom Lumber-Cart more decently would
    hold;
As wise as Calf it look'd, as big as Bully,
But handled, prov'd a mere Sir Nich'las
    Cully;
A bawling Fop, a *nat'ral* Nokes, and yet
He dar'd to *Censure*, to be thought a *Wit*.
To make him more ridiculous, in spight,
Nature contriv'd the Fool should be a Knight.
How wise is *Nature*, when she does dispense
A large Estate, to cover Want of Sense!
From hence unto the upper Walk I ran,
Where a new Scene of Foppery began;
A Tribe of Curates, Priests, Canonical Elves,
Fit Company for none beside themselves,
Were got together; each his Distemper told,
Scurvy, Stone, Strangury; some were so bold
To charge the Spleen to be their Misery,
And on that wise Disease lay Infamy.
But none had Modesty enough t'explain
His Want of Learning, Honesty, or Brain, . . .
Here, waiting for Gallant, young Damsel
    stood,
Leaning on Cane, and muffled up in Hood.
The Would-be-Wit, whose Bus'ness was to
    woe,

With Hat remov'd, and solemn Scrape of
  Shoe,
Advances bowing, then gentilely shrugs,
And ruffled Fore-Top into Order tugs;
And thus accosts her; *Madame, methinks the
  Weather*
Is grown much more serene since you came hither;
You influence the Heav'ns; but should the Sun
Withdraw himself, to see his Rays out-done
By your bright Eyes, They could supply the Morn,
And make a Day, before the Day be born.
With Mouth screw'd up, conceited winking
  Eyes,
And Breast thrust forward, *Lard, Sir*, (she
  replies,)
It is your goodness, and not my Deserts,
Which makes you shew this Learning, Wit, and
  Parts.
He, puzzled, bites his Nails, both to display
The sparkling Ring, and think what next to
  say,
And thus breaks forth afresh; *Madam, Egad,*
Your Luck at Cards Last Night was very bad;
At Cribbidge fifty nine —— and the next Shew,
To make the Game, —— and yet to want those two.
G—d D——, Madam, I'm the Son of a Whore,
If in my Life I saw the like before.

To Pedlar's Stall he drags her, and her Breast,
With Hearts and such like foolish Toys, he
    drest;
And then more smartly to expound the Riddle
Of all this Prattle, gives her a *Scotch* Fiddle.
Tir'd with this dismal Stuff, away I ran,
Faith, I was so asham'd, that with Remorse,
I us'd the Insolence to mount my *Horse*;
For *he*, doing only Things fit for his *Nature*,
Did seem to *me* by much the wiser *Creature*.

John Wilmot, Earl of Rochester (*1647–1680*)
TUNBRIDGE WELLS: A SATIRE

Townsfolk all over England dug furiously in the hope of locating a spring of foul-tasting water which would attract the fashionable world – the *ton* – and make everybody's fortune. An early, though fairly brief, success was made by Epsom, whose burghers located a spring so stiff with chemicals that they were able to produce not only a healing draught but also a crystallised version of the waters which proved to be a sure, rapid and explosive cure for constipation – Epsom Salts.

Tunbridge Wells was the upper-class Spa, much patronised by Nobility. At the other end of the social scale was Epsom, more convenient for London and a favourite haunt of London shopkeepers and their apprentices.

In between these two there were a number of other towns which had been lucky enough to tap a spring within their walls sufficiently sulphurous to attract the *beau monde*, e.g., Buxton, Malvern, Harrogate, Droitwich.

A slightly later but highly successful entry into the Spa racket (which it was) was Cheltenham. Set in a beautiful town the Spa became highly popular amongst the more elegant invalids and rose to even greater heights when it was Graced by the Condescension of a Visit from King George the Third and the Princesses.

What good its waters did was another matter:

> Here lie I and my four daughters,
> Killed by drinking Cheltenham waters.
> Had we but stuck to Epsom salts,
> We wouldn't have been in these here vaults.

Epitaph. Anon.

Cheltenham continued to flourish into the nineteenth century. The kind of people who foregathered there were not at all to the taste of a radical, four-square farmer/journalist/politician who saw it from the back of his horse:

> The Warwickshire Avon falls into the Severn here, and on the sides of both, for many miles back, there are the finest meadows that ever were seen. In looking over them, one wonders *what can become of all the meat?* By riding on about eight or nine miles further, however, this wonder is a little diminished; for here we come to one of the devouring WENS; namely CHELTENHAM, which is what they call a 'watering place'; that is to say, a place to which East India plunderers, West India floggers, English taxgorgers, together with gluttons, drunkards, and debauchees of all descriptions, *female* as well as male, resort, at the suggestion of silently laughing quacks, in the hope of getting rid of the bodily consequences of their manifold sins and iniquities. When I enter a place like this, I always feel disposed to squeeze up my nose with my fingers. It is nonsense, to be sure; but I conceit that every two-legged creature, that I see coming near me, is about to cover me with the poisonous proceeds of its impurities. To places like these come all that is knavish and all that is foolish and all that is base; gamesters, pick-

pockets, and harlots; young wife-hunters in search of rich and ugly and old women, and young husband-hunters in search of rich and wrinkled or half-rotten men, the former resolutely bent, be the means what they may, to give the latter heirs to their lands and tenements. These things are notorious.

William Cobbett (1763–1835)
RURAL RIDES

The Queen of the Spas, however, was the city of Bath. It was the only city which could boast its own hot springs. There had been baths there since Roman times – hence its name – and during the Spa boom it had been put on the map by a visit from Queen Anne. It prospered. Elegant assembly rooms and terraces were built. Beau Nash was appointed the town's Master of Ceremonies and Bath settled down to its business of attracting the wealthy to wallow.

Taking the waters at Bath fell into a regular pattern. As soon as you arrived in town you were announced, in a kind of parody of death, by the tolling of a bell. Everybody who heard the bell knew that further gentry had joined them and quickly sent to know for whom the bell tolled.

The story is taken up by Oliver Goldsmith:

After the family is thus welcomed to *Bath*, it is the custom for the master of it to go to the public places, and subscribe two guineas at the assembly-houses towards the balls and music in the pump-house, for which he is entitled to three tickets every ball night. His next subscription is a crown, half a guinea, or a guinea, according to his rank and quality, for the liberty of walking in the private walks belonging to *Simpson's* assembly-house; a crown or half a guinea is also given to the booksellers, for which the gentleman is to have what books he pleases to read at his lodgings. And at the coffee-house another subscription is taken for pen, ink and paper, for such letters as the subscriber shall write at it during his stay. The ladies too may subscribe to the booksellers, and to an house by the pump-room, for the advantage of reading the news, and for enjoying each other's conversation.

Things being thus adjusted, the amusements of the day are generally begun by bathing, which is no unpleasing method of passing away an hour, or so.

The baths are five in number. On the south-west side of the abbey church is the King's Bath; which is an oblong square, the walls are full of niches, and at every corner are steps to descend into it: this bath is said to contain 427 tons and 50 gallons of water; and on its rising out of the ground over the springs, it is sometimes too hot to be endured by those who bathe therein. Adjoining to the King's Bath there is another, called the Queen's Bath; this is of more temperate warmth, as borrowing its water from the other.

In the south-west part of the city are three other baths, viz. The Hot Bath, which is not much inferior in heat to the King's Bath, and contains 53 tons 2 hogsheads, and 11 gallons of water. The Cross Bath, which contains 52 tons 3 hogsheads, and 11 gallons; and the Leper's Bath, which is not so much frequented as the rest.

The King's Bath (according to the best observations) will fill in about nine hours and a half; the Hot Bath in about eleven hours and a half; and the Cross Bath in about the same time.

The hours for bathing are commonly between six and nine in the morning; and the Baths are every morning supplied with fresh water; for when the people have done bathing, the sluices in each Bath are pulled up, and the water is carried off by drains into the river Avon.

In the morning the lady is brought in a close chair, dressed in her bathing cloaths, to the Bath; and, being in the water, the woman who attends, presents her with a little floating dish like a bason; into which the lady puts an handkerchief, a snuff-box, and a nosegay. She then traverses the Bath; if a novice with a guide, if otherwise by herself; and having amused herself thus while she thinks proper, calls for her chair, and returns to her lodgings.

The amusement of bathing is immediately succeeded by a general assembly of people at the pump-house, some for pleasure, and some to drink the hot waters. Three glasses, at three different times, is the usual portion for every drinker; and the intervals between every glass are enlivened by the harmony of a small band of music, as well as by the conversation of the gay, the witty, or the forward.

From the pump-house the ladies, from time to time, withdraw to a female coffee-house, and from thence return to their lodgings to breakfast. The gentlemen withdraw to their coffee-houses.

Oliver Goldsmith. (1728–1774)
THE LIFE OF RICHARD NASH, OF BATH, ESQ.

One of the publishing successes of the mid-eighteenth century was a poem, in a series of letters, describing a stay at Bath; Christopher Anstey's *The New Bath Guide*. It was issued in 1766 and went through ten editions before the end of the century. Horace Walpole wrote of it to his fri nd Montagu: 'What pleasure you have to come! There is a new thing published that will make you bepiss your cheeks with laughter.' That is, perhaps, rather too large a promise to make

to modern readers but the verse gallops along and the author
agreeably mocks the whole Taking the Cure charade.
   Tabitha is the family's maid:

You cannot conceive what a number of ladies
Were wash'd in the water the same as our maid is:
Old Baron Vanteazer, a man of great wealth,
Brought his Lady, the Baroness, here for her
health;
The Baroness bathes, and she says that her case
Has been hit to a hair, and is mending apace;
And this is a point all the learned agree on,
The Baron has met with the fate of Acteon;
Who, while he peep'd into the bath, had the luck,
To find himself suddenly chang'd to a buck.
Miss Scratchit went in, and the Countess of Scales,
Both ladies of very great fashion in Wales:
Then all on a sudden two ladies of worth,
My Lady Pandora Macscurvy came forth,
With General Sulpher, arrived from the North.
So Tabby, you see, had the honour of washing
With folks of distinction, and very high fashion;
But in spite of good company, poor little soul,
She shook both her ears like a mouse in a bowl.
   Ods-bobs! how delighted I was unawares,
With the fiddles I heard in the room above stairs;
For music is wholesome, the doctors all think,
For ladies that bathe, and for ladies that drink:
And that's the opinion of Robin our driver,
Who whistles his nags while they stand at the river:
They say it is right that for every glass
A tune you should take that the water may pass.
So while little Tabby was washing her rump,
The ladies kept drinking it out of the pump.

Christopher Anstey. (*1724–1805*)
THE NEW BATH GUIDE

Those readers who are passionately devoted to limericks (if there can be any) might be interested to know that 'Roger the lodger', villain of the limerick which finishes 'It wasn't the Almighty Who lifted her nighty, but Roger the lodger the sod', seems to have been inspired by a poem in *The New Bath Guide*.

Miss Prudence informs Lady Betty that she has been elected to Methodism in a dream:

> Blessed I, tho' once rejected,
>   Like a little wand'ring sheep,
> Who this morning was elected
>   By a vision in my sleep.
>
> For I dream'd an apparition
>   Came, like Roger, from above;
> Saying, by divine commission,
>   I must fill you full of love.
>
> Just with Roger's head of hair on,
>   Roger's mouth and pious smile;
> Sweet, methinks, as beard of Aaron,
>   Dropping down with holy oil.
>
> I began to fall a-kicking,
>   Panted, struggled, strove, in vain;
> When the spirit whipt so quick in,
>   I was cur'd of all my pain.
>
> First I thought it was the night-mare
>   Lay so heavy on my breast;
> But I found new joy and light there,
>   When with heav'nly love possest.
>
> Come again then, apparition,
>   Finish what thou has begun;
> Roger, stay! thou soul's physician,
>   I with thee my race will run.

Ibid.

21

Innumerable authors took the waters at Bath and wrote about the experience, including Pope, Fielding, Sheridan, Fanny Burney, Jane Austen, Thackeray and Dickens. Tobias Smollett probably began his *The Expedition of Humphry Clinker* whilst staying there. The irascible Scottish doctor was highly critical of what he saw in the baths, even suggesting that the 'healing fluid' was foul to the taste because visitors were probably drinking the bath water:

I went into the King's Bath, by the advice of our friend Ch———, in order to clear the strainer of the skin, for the benefit of a free perspiration; and the first object that saluted my eye, was a child full of scrophulous ulcers, carried in the arms of one of the guides, under the very noses of the bathers. I was so shocked at the sight, that I retired immediately with indignation and disgust – Suppose the matter of those ulcers, floating on the water, comes in contact with my skin, when the pores are all open, I would ask you what must be the consequence? – Good Heaven, the very thought makes my blood run cold! we know not what sores may be running into the water while we are bathing, and what sort of matter we may thus imbibe; the king's-evil, the scurvy, the cancer, and the pox; and, no doubt, the heat will render the *virus* the more volatile and penetrating.

To purify myself from all such contamination, I went to the duke of Kingston's private Bath, and there I was almost suffocated for want of free air; the place was so small, and the steam so stifling.

After all, if the intention is no more than to wash the skin, I am convinced that simple element is more effectual than any water impregnated with salt and iron; which, being astringent, will certainly contract the pores, and leave a kind of crust upon the surface of the body. But I am now as much afraid of drinking, as of bathing; for, after a long conversation with the Doctor, about the construction of the pump and the cistern, it is very far from being clear with me, that the patients in the Pump-room don't swallow the scourings of the bathers. I can't help suspecting, that there is, or may be, some regurgitation from the bath into the cistern of the pump. In that case, what a delicate beveridge is every day quaffed by the drinkers; medicated with the sweat, and dirt, and dandriff; and the abominable discharges of various kinds, from twenty different diseased bodies, parboiling in the kettle below. In order to avoid this fithy composition, I had recourse to the spring that supplies the private baths on the Abbey-green; but I at once perceived something extraordinary in the taste and smell; and, upon inquiry, I find that the Roman baths in this quarter, were found covered by an old burying ground, belonging to the Abbey; thro' which, in all probability, the water drains in its passage: so that as we drink the decoction of living bodies at the Pump-room, we swallow the strainings of rotten bones and carcasses at the private bath – I vow to God, the very idea turns my stomach!

Tobias Smollett (*1721–1771*)
THE EXPEDITION OF HUMPHRY CLINKER

There is a modern anecdote which illustrates a more recent occasion when bathing and drinking became intertwined.

This story is absolutely true (or, if not true, a lie) and concerns a weekend when Lily Langtry was invited by an Earl to be a guest at his country houseparty. On Saturday morning milord took Miss Langtry aside and asked her whether she would be willing to sport in a bath in view of himself and the other male members of the houseparty, the bath to be filled with a light but sound hock.

Miss Langtry shyly agreed and the rendezvous was fixed at 11 p.m. that evening. At the given time the gentlemen filed solemnly into the mahogany bathroom in the guest wing and puffed silently at their cigars as Miss Langtry, with many a playful shriek, splashed and cavorted in the pale, transparent wine. They then filed out again, busy with their thoughts.

The Earl instructed the butler to rebottle the wine and serve it with the salmon mousse at Sunday luncheon as a fitting tribute to a beautiful and sporting lady. This was done, and the wine – and the gesture – was much appreciated by all.

But that afternoon the butler asked for a word with his master.

'Odd, milord' he said, 'Whereas I poured eight dozen bottles of the Esterhazy-Pierpont-Glückhauser '01 into Miss Langtry's bath – I re-bottled eight dozen bottles and one half'.

Probably the last examples of the large communal bath, endured for social and medicinal reasons for so many centuries, are municipal swimming-pools and a few institutional baths still used in some establishments as a cheap and simple method of getting batches of small boys, if not clean, at least wet:

> And there was the slimy water of the plunge
> bath – it was twelve or fifteen feet long, the whole
> school was supposed to go into it every morning,
> and I doubt whether the water was changed at all
> frequently – and the always-damp towels with
> their cheesy smell: and, on occasional visits in the
> winter, the murky sea-water of the local Baths,
> which came straight in from the beach and on
> which I once saw floating a human turd. And the
> sweaty smell of the changing-room with its greasy
> basins, and, giving on this, the row of filthy,
> dilapidated lavatories, which had no fastenings of
> any kind on the doors, so that whenever you were
> sitting there someone was sure to come crashing
> in. It is not easy for me to think of my schooldays
> without seeming to breathe in a whiff of something
> cold and evil-smelling – a sort of compound of
> sweaty stockings, dirty towels, faecal smells
> blowing along corridors, forks with old food
> between the prongs, neck-of-mutton stew, and the
> banging doors of the lavatories and the echoing
> chamber-pots in the dormitories.

George Orwell (*1903–1950*)
SUCH, SUCH WERE THE JOYS

Most hot-country religions laid down elaborate rules of hygiene. Ancient Eastern races and tribes, when they first came up against Western travellers, were horrified by their filthy habits: We did have *some* rules, of course:

> Wash your hands often, your feet seldom, your head never.
>
> English proverb. Sixteenth century.

And it was said, with considerable pride, that Queen Elizabeth I bathed once a month 'whether she needed it or no'.

Royalty and nobility frequently had elaborate baths constructed for their use but, of course, there was little or no plumbing to get the water in and take it away again. The water had to be warmed and poured in from jugs, like a marble version of a miner's galvanised iron tub. Bathing was a rare ritual event.

Some ladies preferred the simplicity of a dip in the river. One such dip inflamed a poet who wrote the lucky river a small ode:

> How fierce was I when I did see
> My Julia wash herself in thee!
> So lilies thorough crystal look,
> So purest pebbles in the brook,
> As in the river Julia did,
> Half with a lawn of water hid.
> Into thy stream myself I threw
> And struggling there I kissed thee too;
> And more had done, it is confessed,
> Had not the waves forbade the rest
>
> Robert Herrick (*1591–1674*)
> UPON JULIA'S WASHING HERSELF IN THE RIVER

The Marquise de Saint-Hérem, a slightly dotty French lady of the Court of Louis XIV, had an idea for making her dip in the river more agreeable. It was not a very good idea:

> She once succeeded in boiling her own leg in the middle of the River Seine, near Fontainebleau. The water had proved too cold for her liking when she was bathing, and she had had large quantities heated on the bank and poured around and over her, with the result that she was severely scalded and remained housebound for a week. In thunderstorms she had a habit of going down on all fours under her day-bed, and obliging her servants to lie piled on top of her, so that the thunder might lose its effect before it reached her.

> Duc de Saint-Simon (1675–1755)
HISTORICAL MEMOIRS. Translated by Lucy Norton

What with one hazard and another, bathing seems to have been quite dangerous. The Dowager Duchess of Norfolk's great height almost provoked a catastrophe:

> The Dowager Duchess of Norfolk bathes, and being very tall she had like to have drowned a few women in the Cross Bath, for she ordered it to be filled till it reached to her chin, and so all those who were below her stature, as well as rank, were forced to come out or drown.

> Elizabeth Montagu (1720–1800)
Letter to the Duchess of Portsmouth

A French Queen also got into difficulties:

> In this room there are several portraits of the French family, including pictures of the French Queen herself and of her husband Louis Philippe. Next door was her dressing room with a deep large bath, almost concealed, in which the old French

Queen was nearly drowned. Her attendant had left
her for a few minutes and when she returned the
old Queen was struggling and plunging about in
the bath almost at her last gasp.

Rev. Francis Kilvert (*1840–1879*)
DIARY Wed. 18 Jan. 1871

A bit of interest in bathing grew in the eighteenth century,
partly because people in the Age of Reason tended to be
enthusiastic about anything which could be called scientific,
and partly because they were obsessed with their health and
they came to believe that immersion in water was good for the
body. Cold baths, it seems, were a sovereign specific against
that widespread complaint – melancholia:

> The cold Bath which I have gone into for three
> weeks past have quite recovered my weak nerves
> and restored me to good Spirits and the Blew
> Devils are quite gone away, not, I suppose, very
> well relishing the cold water.

Lord Dacre
Letter to Sanderson Miller, May 1745

They wrote poems and inscriptions about, and upon,
practically everything in that century. William Whitehead,
anxious to get the drooping patient into cold water once
med'cine had failed and balms and herbs essay'd their powers
in vain, wrote a poem to be inscribed on the side of the bath:

Whoe'er thou art, approach – Has med'cine
fail'd?
Have balms and herbs essay'd their powers
in vain?
Nor the free air, nor fost'ring Sun prevail'd
To raise thy drooping strength, or soothe
thy pain?

Yet enter here. Nor doubt to trust thy frame
  To the cold bosom of this lucid lake.
Here Health may greet thee, and life's
    languid flame,
  Ev'n from its icy grasp, new vigour take.

What soft Ausonia's genial shores deny,
  May Zembla give. Then boldly trust the
    wave:
So shall thy grateful tablet hang on high,
  And frequent votaries bless this healing
    cave.

William Whitehead (<i>1715–1785</i>)
INSCRIPTION FOR A COLD BATH

A superb example of an eighteenth-century didactic poem is *The Art of Preserving Health*, an extremely long, book-length poem telling the reader where it is healthiest to live, what to eat, etc., in blank verse so stately and rich that some passages have to be read many times with the help of a classical dictionary and the full-size O.E.D. before much of a message emerges.

In the following extract the poet, Dr. Armstrong, has something favourable to say about 'the gelid cistern' (the cold bath):

> Against the rigours of a damp cold heav'n
> To fortify our bodies, some frequent
> The gelid cistern; and, where none forbids,
> I praise their dauntless heart. A frame so steel'd
> Dreads not the cough, nor those ungenial blasts,
> That breathe the Tertian or fell Rheumatism;
> The Nerves so temper'd never quit their tone,
> No chronic langours haunt such hardy breasts . . .

29

Then he goes on a bit about 'the safe vicissitudes of life' which I do not wholly understand, and a passage 'ill-fitted he to want the known, or bear unusual things' which I do not understand at all. Then the mists clear and we find the poet advising global travellers to take three warm baths a day:

> Let those who from the frozen Arctos reach
> Parch'd Mauritania, or the sultry West,
> Or the wide flood that waters Indostan,
> Plunge thrice a day, and in the tepid wave
> Untwist their stubborn pores; that full and free
> Th' evaporation thro' the softened skin
> May bear proportion to the swelling blood.
> So shall they 'scape the fever's rapid flames;
> So feel untainted the hot breath of hell.
> With us, the man of no complaint demands
> The warm ablution, just enough to clear
> The sluices of the skin, enough to keep
> The body sacred from indecent soil.

John Armstrong M.D. (*1769–1779*)
THE ART OF PRESERVING HEALTH

It is no wonder that, apart from health cranks, hardly anybody at that time 'frequented the gelid cistern'. In his account of Samuel Johnson's middle years, James. L. Clifford describes what life was like without baths:

> But now back to Johnson's everyday life in the simple but commodious house in Gough Square. One may easily guess where Johnson and Tetty slept, but more perplexing problems have to do with sanitation and cleanliness. When Johnson wanted to wash his face, where did he find the water? And what happened to the dirty water after he was through? When he took a bath, if he ever did, where was the tub? In the bedroom? Or in the basement kitchen near one of the large fireplaces? And what happened to the contents of his chamber

pots? There are no references to such mundane matters in surviving diary entries or letters. All we can do is speculate, using such evidence as has come to light.

In 1749 in Gough Square there were certainly no bathrooms or running water. No ordinary London house at that time had bathrooms, and hardly any nobleman's. When Johnson and Tetty washed it was undoubtedly in a china bowl, with water from a nearby pitcher. By mid-century most houses on major streets did have leaden pipes bearing water from conduits coming into the basement or kitchen, but the water was turned on for short periods only three times a week. Thus the house-holder had to have a cistern or tank in the basement where water could be stored. For those without pipes the contents could be replenished by rain-water from gutters on the roof. And there were water carriers in most parts of London. Since Johnson did not live directly on a major street, it is unlikely that his house was supplied with pipes from the outside. In any case, water had to be carried upstairs by servants in pitchers or buckets, one explanation of the small size of portable tubs and the infrequency of bathing.

James L. Clifford (*1901–1979*)
DICTIONARY JOHNSON

It seems unlikely that the absence of washing facilities bothered Samuel Johnson. He did not regard personal cleanliness as being of much importance:

[of Kit Smart]
'He did not love clean linen, and I have no passion for it.'

Boswell's LIFE. 24 May, 1763

31

Boswell was more nattily dressed than Johnson but, it seems, was equally unwashed:

> 'James Boswell, the faithful biographer of Dr.
> Johnson, meeting him in the pit of the Pantheon,
> loudly exclaimed, "Why, Nollekens, how dirty
> you go now! I recollect when you were the gayest
> dressed of any in the house." To whom Nollekens
> made, for once in his life, the retort-courteous of
> "That's more than I could ever say of you!"
> Boswell certainly looked very badly when dressed;
> for, as he seldom washed himself, his clean ruffles
> served as a striking contrast to his dirty flesh.'
>
> J. T. Smith (*1766–1833*)
> NOLLEKENS AND HIS TIME

For something like a hundred years after Johnson most baths were not plumbed in and those which were had only cold water on tap and usually had no waste-pipe. This dependence on a bath being filled from a hand-held jug tempted some eccentrics to bath in fluids other than water. Beau Brummel claimed that he bathed in milk but offered no proof. It is more readily believable of 'Old Q' the archetypal dissolute nobleman. Unfortunately for the dairy industry in London a rumour grew that the milk sold in the capital was recycled:

> 'There are many persons still living who
> remember the almost universal prejudice against
> drinking milk which prevailed in the metropolis, in
> consequence of its being supposed that this
> common necessary of life might have been retailed
> from the daily lavations of the Duke of
> Queensberry.'
>
> J. H. Jesse (*1815–1874*)
> GEORGE SELWYN AND HIS CONTEMPORARIES

Showers (cold-water only) came into use in the nineteenth century, although Dr. Routh could see little point in installing them in his Oxford college for, as he pointed out, undergraduates were only in residence for eight weeks at a stretch.

A shower took up much less room in a bedroom than did a bath and was cheaper. Servants would have to mop up a wider area of carpet but would have to carry down less volume of dirty water.

There was one snag, and that a nasty one – the shock to the nervous system when the cord was pulled and the icy needles hit warm flesh:

> Trembling, as Father Adam stood
> To pull the stalk, before the Fall,
> So stand I here, before the Flood,
> On my own head the shock to call:
> How like our predecessor's luck!
> 'Tis but to pluck – but needs some pluck!
>
> Still thoughts of gasping like a pup
> Will paralyze the nervous pow'r;
> Now hoping it will yet hold up,
> Invoking now the tumbling show'r; –
> But, ah! the shrinking body loathes,
> Without a parapluie or clothes!
>
> 'Expect some rain about this time!'
> My eyes are seal'd, my teeth are set –
> But where's the Stoic so sublime
> Can ring, unmov'd, for wringing wet?
> Of going hogs some folks talk big –
> Just let them try *the whole cold pig*!

Tom Hood (*1799–1845*)
STANZAS, COMPOSED IN A SHOWER-BATH

The nerve required for a person to turn on a cold shower proved too much for many people, including, it is shameful to relate, a pillar of Britain's political establishment. Mrs. Disraeli confided to friends:

> 'Dizzy has the most wonderful moral courage in
> the world, but no physical courage. When he uses
> his shower-bath, I always have to pull the string.'
>
> G. W. E. Russell (*1853–1919*)
> A POCKETFUL OF SIXPENCES

Of sterner stuff was a country parson. Unlike a cold shower, with its instant impact, a cold bath can be entered gingerly, a toe at a time, and withdrawn from instantly should gangrene or stoppage of the heart seem imminent.

All the same. Not much of a start to vicar's Christmas morning:

> As I lay awake praying in the early morning I
> thought I heard a sound of distant bells. It was an
> intense frost. I sat down in my bath upon a sheet of
> thick ice which broke in the middle into large
> pieces whilst sharp points and jagged edges stuck
> all round the sides of the tub like chevaux de frise,
> not particularly comforting to the naked thighs and
> loins, for the keen ice cut like broken glass. The
> ice water stung and scorched like fire. I had to
> collect the floating pieces of ice and pile them on a
> chair before I could use the sponge and then I had
> to thaw the sponge in my hands for it was a mass of
> ice. The morning was most brilliant.
>
> Rev. Francis Kilvert (*1840–1879*)
> DIARY Sunday, December 25, 1870

A significant point which has probably already occurred to the reader is that nobody so far in their diaries and journals and poems has mentioned using the bath for the purpose of scrubbing the body.

The Romans used their baths mainly as social clubs, the cleaning process being a dubious system whereby they were massaged with oils which were squeegeed off by a slave with a *strigil*, a flesh-scraper.

During the dark centuries that followed perhaps the only people who bathed more than once or twice a year were monks in monasteries and, again, it was sitting in water which was the objective; there is little mention of scrubbing or indeed cleansing the sullied flesh.

The old Roman system of using oil – rather like cleaning a bicycle – was still current in the seventeenth century among the nobility, according to Francis Bacon. His instructions on how to take a bath read more like a course in Do-It-Yourself embalming:

First, before bathing, rub and anoint the Body with Oyle, and Salves, that the Bath's moistening heate and virtue may penetrate into the Body, and not the liquor's watery part: then sit 2 houres in the Bath; after Bathing wrap the Body in a seare-cloth made of Masticke, Myrrh, Pomander and Saffron, for staying the perspiration or breathing of the pores, until the softening of the Body, having layne thus in seare-cloth 24 houres, bee growne solid and hard. Lastly, with an oyntment of Oyle, Salt and Saffron, the seare-cloth being taken off, anoint the Body.

Francis Bacon, Baron Verulam (*1561–1626*)
SYLVA SYLVARUM

For the next two hundred years most citizens did not bath

at all. In hot Assembly Rooms and at the card tables this became something of a problem, which was solved by using scent, as did the Romans; 'a smell to cover a stink'.

The Age of Elegance, the eighteenth century, might have delighted the eye with its architecture and its fine fashions, and the ear with its music, but it must have been deeply offensive to the nose.

Then, early in the nineteenth century, a complete change came about. The British decided, for the first time in history, that washing was a good thing. And bathing was even better. Soap, used in previous centuries mainly for washing clothes and scrubbing the kitchen table, became heavily advertised and available commercially in a range of smells, from 'musk' to the hugely popular and reassuring odour of disinfectant, 'coal-tar'.

Ignoring the teachings of the early Christian leaders – St. Francis of Assisi taught that dirtiness was an indication of holiness, St. Jerome was ashamed of his followers for being too clean, St. Catherine of Siena gave up washing for good, St. Agnes died without ever having washed – the Victorians decided that washing was not only socially desirable but also highly pious. In support of this claim they made a line from one of John Wesley's sermons into a popular slogan: Cleanliness is next to Godliness:

> it is odd that the English
>   a rather dirty people
>   should have invented the slogan
> *Cleanliness is next to Godliness*
>   meaning by that
>   a gentleman smells faintly of tar
> persuaded themselves that constant cold
> hydropathy
>   would make the sons of gentlemen
> pure in heart
>   (not that papa or his chilblained offspring can
>   hope to be gentry)
>   still John Bull's

```
hip-bath it was
                 that made one carnal pleasure
lawful
       for the first time since we quarrelled
over Faith and Works
                       (Shakespeare probably stank
                                    Le Grand
Monarque certainly did)...
```

W. H. Auden (1907–1973)
ENCOMIUM BALNEI

John Wesley preached his sermon in the middle of the eighteenth century, perhaps the point when personal hygiene in Britain was at its lowest and parsons might be expected to scratch as they preached and dig around in their wigs with a quill to shift the lice about a bit. Why should he suddenly declare to his congregation that personal hygiene was a saintly virtue?

A glance at the text of Wesley's sermon reveals that he was not talking about personal cleanliness at all. He was warning his followers against wearing scruffy clothes:

L et it be observed, that slovenliness is no part of religion; that neither this, nor any text of Scripture, condemns neatness of apparel. Certainly this is a duty, not a sin. 'Cleanliness is, indeed, next to godliness'.

John Wesley (1703–1791)
SERMONS, No. xciii, ON DRESS

Wesley was clearly quoting an old saying. Brewer's Dictionary believes the phrase to have come from the writings of Phinehas ben Yair, an ancient Hebrew rabbi.

As the nineteenth century advanced, the new-found pleasure – now a duty – of soaping oneself and wallowing in a bath, or cringing under a shower, spread rapidly among those who could afford the soap and the ironmongery.

Leaps in technology brought water to increasing numbers of town houses and an urgent need to improve the drains meant that more baths and showers could be piped into the sewage system.

Manufacturers offered an increasingly bewildering range of reasonably priced baths in many materials, cast-iron, copper, papier-mâché, and in an assortment of designs; sponge baths, sitz baths, slipper baths, hip baths, and so on.

The British had, at last, become a nation of bathers, of wielders of soap and flannel.

Authorities on matters of health still urged caution, clinging to the old eighteenth-century attitude that baths were for therapeutic purposes only and should be on a doctor's prescription:

3523. BATHS AND BATHING.

The frequency with which a bath should be repeated varies somewhat with different individuals. A safe rule, to which of course there are sundry exceptions, would be to bathe the body twice a week in winter and every other day in summer, gradually increasing the frequency to a tri-weekly washing in winter and a daily one in summer, if experience proves that better health is secured by such a habit.

3524. HOT BATHS by which are meant those of a temperature of from 85° to 105° Fahrenheit, are chiefly used in the treatment of diseases as powerful stimulants. Every parent should remember that a hot bath, causing free perspiration, promoted by wrapping up warm in bed with blankets, will often save children and adults severe attacks of illness, if promptly resorted to after exposure to cold or wet.

3526. COLD BATHS are invaluable aids in promoting and preserving health, if properly used in suitable cases; but may become dangerous agents, causing even fatal results, if employed by the wrong individuals, at improper times, or with excessive frequency.

Baths should never be taken immediately after a meal, nor when the body is very much exhausted by fatigue or excitement of any kind, nor during nor just before menstruation; and they should be sparingly and guardedly used by pregnant women.

Mrs. Isabella Beeton (*1836–1865*)
HOUSEHOLD MANAGEMENT

Throughout the nineteenth century new comforts and facilities became available to the bather. Perhaps the most welcome was the happy combination of piped gas and piped water which made possible the invention of the geyser. At last it was no longer necessary to warm up the bath with jugs of hot water. The bather could have a bath at any temperature he or she desired:

I test my bath before I sit,
And I'm always moved to wonderment
That what chills the finger not a bit
Is so frigid upon the fundament.

Ogden Nash (*1902–1971*)

Unlike the old sitz and hip baths which were carried into the bedroom when needed and whisked away afterwards, the new baths were massive and permanent:

The enormous mahogany-sided bath was approached by two steps, and had a sort of grotto containing a shower-bath at one end; this was lined with as many different stops as the organ in King's Chapel. And it was as difficult to control as it

would be for an amateur to play that organ.
Piercing jets of boiling, or ice-cold, water came
roaring at one from the most unexpected angles,
and hit one in the tenderest spots.

Gwen Raverat (*1885–1957*)
PERIOD PIECE: A CAMBRIDGE CHILDHOOD

In great houses a bedroom or dressing-room in the guest
wing would be nominated the 'bathroom' and be suitably
adapted.

When Charles revisited Brideshead he was always given the
bedroom he had on his first visit:

It was next to Sebastian's, and we shared what had
once been a dressing-room and had been changed
to a bathroom twenty years back by the
substitution for the bed of a deep, copper,
mahogany-framed bath, that was filled by pulling a
brass lever heavy as a piece of marine engineering;
the rest of the room remained unchanged; a coal
fire always burned there in winter. I often think of
that bathroom – the water colours dimmed by
steam and the huge towel warming on the back of
the chintz armchair – and contrast it with the
uniform, clinical, little chambers, glittering with
chromium-plate and looking-glass, which pass for
luxury in the modern world.

Evelyn Waugh (*1903–1966*)
BRIDESHEAD REVISITED

The converted dressing-room or bedroom, with its fireplace
and its chintz, would also have had plenty of cupboard space:

Miss Twye was soaping her breasts in her bath
When she heard behind her a meaning laugh
And to her amazement she discovered
A wicked man in the bathroom cupboard.

Gavin Ewart (*1916–   *)
MISS TWYE

The ex-bedroom would also have contained a mirror, probably a tall pier-glass large enough for the whole figure to be viewed and the dress or suit twitched and smoothed before going down to dinner.

As late as the 1950s a Bishop, staying as a guest in a large house, took a bath, skipped out of it and was appalled to see, in a large-pier glass which he had not noticed before, the reflection of his body stark naked.

He expressed his shock and dismay.

A poet replied:

> Beneath that Chasuble, my Lord, that holds
> You close (as Charity all men enfolds);
> Beneath that Cope that, opening before,
> Of Life Eternal signifies the Door,
> And (as Durandus taught) recalls the strength
> Of godly Perseverance by its length;
> Beneath that Rochet of pure lawn, and whiter
> Than Iceland's winter cap; beneath that Mitre;
> A body stands concealed, which God once chose
> The Spirits of his Children to enclose,
> And (as a Bishop surely must believe)
> His Very Self Incarnate to receive.
> Yet, through a mirror suddenly aware
> That 'Temples of the Spirit' can be bare,
> You shrink aghast, with pained and puzzled eyes,
> While God's great laughter peals about the skies.

Sir Lawrence Jones (*1885–1969*)
LINES TO A BISHOP WHO WAS SHOCKED (A.D. 1950)
AT SEEING A PIER-GLASS IN A BATHROOM

During the early years of the twentieth century a great many of the huge mansions in the inner suburbs of London were split up into flats to house the growing army of office workers. It was necessary to provide proper bathing facilities for the bed-sitters and flat-dwellers who now occupied the houses and so tiny bathrooms were built on each landing. Passengers on trains dawdling into the terminus can look up

at the back of these old mansions and see these bathrooms,
like little brick huts stuck to the wall:

> From the geyser ventilators
>   Autumn winds are blowing down
> On a thousand business women
>   Having baths in Camden Town.
>
> Waste pipes chuckle into runnels,
>   Steam's escaping here and there,
> Morning trains through Camden cutting
>   Shake the Crescent and the Square.
>
> Early nip of changeful autumn,
>   Dahlias glimpsed through garden doors,
> At the back precarious bathrooms
>   Jutting out from upper floors;
>
> And behind their frail partitions
>   Business women lie and soak,
> Seeing through the draughty skylight
>   Flying clouds and railway smoke.
>
> Rest you there, poor unbelov'd ones,
>   Lap your loneliness in heat.
> All too soon the tiny breakfast,
>   Trolley-bus and windy street!

John Betjeman (*1906–*)
BUSINESS GIRLS

The notion of the modern bathroom, a small hygienic cell
into which was tightly packed the bath, wash-basin, bathroom
cabinet and mirror, and the W.C., an idea which Americans
pioneered, gradually became the accepted thing in Britain.

It was a triumph of ingenious and complicated plumbing.
And with complicated plumbing, and winter, came the
plumber:

Plumber is icumen in;
Bludie big tu-du.
Bloweth lampe, and showeth dampe,
And dripth the wud thru.
Bludie hel, boo-hoo!

Thawth drain, and runneth bath;
Saw sawth, and scruth scru;
Bull-kuk squirteth, leakë spurteth;
Wurry springeth up anew,
Boo-hoo, boo-hoo.

Tom Pugh, Tom Pugh, well plumbës thu, Tom
    Pugh;
Better job I naver nu.
Therefore will I cease boo-hoo,
Woorie not, but cry pooh-pooh,
Murie sing pooh-pooh, pooh-pooh,
Pooh-pooh!

A. Y. Campbell (1885–1958)
POEMS

This new network of up-pipes, down-pipes and assorted spouts on the exterior of buildings, according to a poet, proved a hazard to fauna:

We 'ad a bleed'n' sparrer wot
Lived up a bleed'n' spaht,
One day the bleed'n' rain came dahn
An' washed the bleeder aht.

An' as 'e layed 'arf drahnded
Dahn in the bleed'n street
'E begged that bleed'n' rainstorm
To bave 'is bleed'n' feet.

But then the bleed'n' sun came aht –
Dried up the bleed'n' rain –
So that bleed'n' little sparrer
'E climbed up 'is spaht again.

43

But, Oh! – the crewel sparrer'awk,
'E spies 'im in 'is snuggery,
'E sharpens up 'is bleed'n' claws
An' rips 'im aht by thuggery!

Jist then a bleed'n' sportin' type
Wot 'ad a bleed'n' gun
'E spots that bleed'n' sparrer'awk
An' blasts 'is bleed'n' fun.

The moral of this story
Is plain to everyone –
That them wot's up the bleed'n' spaht
Don't get no bleed'n' fun.

Anon

Perhaps the surest sign of the way that bathing had become a part of the daily domestic routine was the frequency with which it was mentioned in contemporary literature:

Mr. Salteena woke up rather early next day and was surprised and delighted to find Horace the footman entering with a cup of tea.

Oh thankyou my man said Mr. Salteena rolling over in the costly bed. Mr. Clark is nearly out of the bath sir anounced Horace I will have great plesure in turning it on for you if such is your desire. Well yes you might said Mr. Salteena seeing it was the idear and Horace gave a profound bow.

Ethel are you getting up shouted Mr. Salteena.

Very nearly replied Ethel faintly from the next room.

I say said Mr. Salteena excitedly I have had some tea in bed.

So have I replied Ethel.

Then Mr. Salteena got into a mouve dressing goun with yellow tassles and siezing his soap he wandered off to the bath room which was most sumpshous. It had a lovly white shiny bath and sparkling taps and several towels arrayed in readiness by thourghtful Horace. It also had a step for climbing up the bath and other good dodges of a rich nature. Mr. Salteena washed himself well and felt very much better.

Daisy Ashford (*1881–1972*)
THE YOUNG VISITERS

However, even well into the twentieth century not everybody could afford to install bathrooms with dodges of a rich nature. To many people installing a bathroom with even modest dodges was a luxury:

Yesterday I heard from Harcourt Brace that Mrs. D. & C.R. are selling 148 and 73 weekly – Isn't that a surprising rate for the 4th month? Doesn't it portend a bathroom & w.c. either here or Southease? ...

Virginia Woolf (*1882–1941*)
DIARY 22 Sept. 1925. ed: Anne Olivier Bell

In rural areas it was still unusual to find a bath in a cottage. The gentry may have had their bathrooms but the village folk made do:

Although only babies and very small children had baths, the hamlet folk were cleanly in their persons. The women would lock their doors for the whole afternoon once a week to have what they called 'a good clean-up'. This consisted of stripping to the waist and washing downward; then stepping into a footbath and washing upward. 'Well, I feels all the better for that,' some woman would say complacently. 'I've washed up as far as possible and down as far as possible,' and the

45

ribald would inquire what poor 'possible' had done
that it should not be included.

Flora Thompson (*1877–1947*)
LARK RISE TO CANDLEFORD, 1945.

Even the most genteel wash was accomplished with a huge
jug of water and a basin which usually sat upon the
'washstand' in the bedroom.

This had to suffice even for the lady's stripped-to-the-waist
ablution so happily painted by Degas and lovingly described
by D. H. Lawrence:

> When she rises in the morning
> I linger to watch her;
> She spreads the bath-cloth underneath the window
> And the sunbeams catch her
> Glistening white on the shoulders,
> While down her sides the mellow
> Golden shadow glows as
> She stoops to the sponge, and her swung breasts
> Sway like full-blown yellow
> Gloire de Dijon roses.

D. H. Lawrence (*1885–1930*)
GLOIRE DE DIJON

It was a less poetic and more difficult procedure for the
Rev. Wm. Archibald Spooner, Warden of New College,
Oxford, whose mind was habitually absent from what he was
doing at any given moment:

> Spooner was meditating ablution and had lifted a
> full jug of water from the wash-hand stand, where
> a basin also stood ready. Something that was
> passing through his mind caused him to walk, jug
> in hand, to the window. Then remembering his
> original purpose, he emptied the jug – but onto a
> passing undergraduate below.
> 'Warden, Warden!' the undergraduate cried out.

'Why did you do that?'
   Spooner replied:
'Why are you in my basin?'

Quoted by T. F. Higham, M.A. (*1890–1975*)
A BOOK OF ANECDOTES

Among working folk in towns, too, baths were a novelty. Even when a landlord installed one it was seldom taken seriously:

'And a loovly bath where we can keep the coal . . .'

Will E. Haines and Jimmy Harper, 1928
IN MY LITTLE BOTTOM DRAWER
Performed by Gracie Fields

Miners, after their day's work at the coal face, traditionally soaped themselves clean in a tin bath in front of the kitchen fire:

With a look at the clock – the first thing Sammy had got out of pawn for her – she pulled the tin bath before the fire and began to fill it with hot water from the wash-house.

The clock struck five, and shortly after the tramp of feet echoed along the Terrace, the slow tramp of tired men. Nine hours from bank to bank and the Terraces to climb at the end of it. But it was good honest work, bred in their bones, and in her bones too. Her sons were young and strong. It was their work. She desired no other.

The door opened upon her thought and the three came in, Hughie first, then David, and finally Sammy with a sawn balk of timber tucked under his arm, for her kindling.

'How, mother,' Sammy smiled, his teeth showing white against the black coal dust that sweat had caked on him.

She loved the way he called her mother, not that 'mam' in common usage here; but she merely

47

nodded towards the bath that was ready and turned back to set the table.

With their mother in the room the three lads took off their boots, jackets, their pit drawers and singlets, all sodden with water, sweat and pit dirt. Together, naked to the buff, they stood scouring themselves in the tiny steaming bath. There was never much room and it was always friendly. But there was not much joking to-night. Sam in a tentative way nudged Davey and grinned: 'Ower the bed a bit, ye elephant.' And again remarked: 'Whey, mon, have ye swallowed the soap?' But there was nothing genuine in the way of fun. The heaviness in the house, in Martha's face, precluded it. They dressed with no horse-play, sat in to their dinner almost in silence.

A. J. Cronin (*1896–1980*)
THE STARS LOOK DOWN

The miner in a novel by Emile Zola fared more happily. Well, he was married and what with all that soaping . . . They order, it seems, this matter better in France –

The tub was refilled with warm water and father was beginning to take off his jacket. A warning glance was the signal for Alzire to take Lénore and Henri to play outside. Dad did not like bathing in front of the family, as they did in many other homes in the village. Not that he was criticising anybody; he only meant that dabbling about together was all right for children.

'What are you doing up there?' Maheude called up the stairs.

'Mending my dress that I tore yesterday,' Catherine called back.

'All right, but don't come down; your father's washing.'

Maheu and his wife were alone. She had made

up her mind to put Estelle down in a chair as, for a wonder, she was not yelling, being near the fire. She gazed at her parents with the expressionless eyes of a tiny creature without intelligence. He crouched naked in front of the tub and began by dipping his head in, well lathered with soft soap. The use of this soap for generations past had discoloured the hair of all these people and turned it yellow. Then he stepped into the water, soaped his chest, belly, arms, and legs and rubbed them hard with his fists. His wife stood looking on.

'Well,' she began, 'I saw the look on your face when you came in. You were feeling pretty worried, weren't you? And the sight of the food cheered you up no end. Just fancy, those gentry up at La Piolaine never coughed up a sou. Of course, they were very nice – they gave the kids some clothes and I was ashamed to beg. It sticks in my throat when I have to cadge.'

She broke off to settle Estelle firmly in the chair, for fear she might topple over. Father went on pummelling his skin, without trying to hurry the story by asking questions. It interested him, but he patiently waited for things to be made plain.

'I must tell you that Maigrat had turned me down flat, like turning a dog out. You can imagine what a nice time I had. Woollen clothes may be all right for keeping you warm, but they don't fill your stomach, do they?'

He looked up, but still said nothing. Nothing from La Piolaine, nothing from Maigrat: well, what? But she was going on with the usual routine, having rolled her sleeves up so as to do his back and the places that are hard to get at. Anyway, he loved her to soap him and rub him all over fit to break her wrists. She took some soap and worked away at his shoulders, while he stiffened his body to withstand the attack.

49

'So back I went to Maigrat's and told him the tale. Oh, I didn't half tell him the tale! Said he couldn't have any heart, that he would come to a bad end if there was any justice in the world. He didn't like that at all, and he rolled his eyes round and would have liked to skedaddle....'

She had gone down from his back to his buttocks and, warming up to the job, she pushed ahead into the cracks and did not leave a single part of his body untouched, making it shine like her three saucepans on spring-cleaning Saturdays. But the terrible arm-work made her sweat, shook her and took her breath away, so that her words came in gasps.

'Anyway, he called me an old limpet.... We've got enough bread till Saturday, and the best of it is that he lent me five francs. What's more, I got the butter, coffee, and chicory from him and was going to buy the meat and potatoes, but I saw he was beginning to jib.... Seven sous for the brawn, eighteen for the potatoes, that leaves me three francs seventy-five for a stew and some boiled beef. I haven't wasted my morning, have I, eh?'

She was now drying him, dabbing with a towel at the places that were difficult to dry. He, happy and carefree about the morrow's debts, laughed out loud and threw his arms round her.

'Don't be silly! You have made me all wet! Only.... I'm afraid Maigrat had got something in mind....'

She was on the point of mentioning Catherine, but checked herself. Why upset father? It would start off an endless fuss.

'Got what in mind?'

'Oh, only how to swindle us. Catherine will have to go over the bill carefully.'

He seized her again, and this time did not leave

go. The bath always ended up like this – she made him excited by rubbing so hard and then towelling him everywhere, tickling the hairs on his arms and chest. It was the time when all the chaps in the village took their fun and more children were planted than anybody wanted. At night they had their families in the way. He pushed her to the table, cracking jokes to celebrate the one good moment a chap can enjoy during the whole day, calling it taking his dessert – and free of charge, what's more! She, with her flabby body and breasts hanging all over the place, put up a bit of resistance, just for fun.

'You silly, you! Oh, you are a one! And there's Estelle looking at us! Wait a minute while I turn her head the other way.'

'Oh, rubbish! What does she understand at three months?'

When it was over, he put on just a dry pair of trousers.

Emile Zola (*1840–1902*)
GERMINAL trans.: Leonard Tancock

To the inhabitants of hot and sunny Mediterranean islands the modern English preoccupation with personal hygiene was put down to diabolism or hypochondria:

English eccentricity remarked by the natives which the Count has missed; the English demand for houses with lavatories. An 'English' house in the island, has come to mean a house with a lavatory; and the landlord of such a house will charge almost double the ordinary rent for so remarkable an innovation. Bathrooms are even rarer and are considered a dangerous and rather satanic contrivance. For the peasants a bath is something you are sometimes forced to take by the doctor as a medicinal measure; the idea of cleanliness does not enter into it. Theodore often quotes the old peasant who reverently crossed himself when shown the fine tiled bathroom at the Count's country house and said: 'Pray God, my Lord, that you will never need it.'

Lawrence Durrell (*1912*–)
PROSPERO'S CELL

It was only when bathrooms were present in almost all homes, ceased to be a novelty and were taken for granted, that there emerged the fact that mankind had created for itself a number of new dangers. Bathrooms, because of what they contained and what they were used for, presented a range of new ways in which the human species could do itself damage. There was the fearful danger of bathing a slender child in a bath with a wide plug-hole:

A muvver was barfin' 'er biby one night,
The youngest of ten and a tiny young mite,
The muvver was poor and the biby was thin,
Only a skelington covered in skin;
The muvver turned rahnd for the soap off the rack,
She was but a moment, but when she turned back,
The biby was gorn; and in anguish she cried,
'Oh, where is my biby?' – The angels replied:

'Your biby 'as fell dahn the plug-'ole,
Your biby 'as gorn dahn the plug;
The poor little thing was so skinny and thin
'E oughter been barfed in a jug;
Your biby is perfeckly 'appy,
'E won't need a barf any more,
Your biby 'as fell dahn the plug-'ole,
Not lorst, but gorn before.'

Anon.

And witness the disasters which befell Mr. Pooter when he decided to paint his bath:

APRIL 25. In consequence of Brickwell telling me his wife was working wonders with the new Pinkford's enamel paint, I determined to try it. I bought two tins of red on my way home. I hastened through tea, went into the garden and painted some flower-pots. I called out Carrie, who said: 'You've always got some new-fangled craze'; but she was obliged to admit that the flower-pots looked remarkably well. Went upstairs into the servant's bedroom and painted her washstand, towel-horse, and chest of drawers. To my mind it was an extraordinary improvement, but as an example of the ignorance of the lower classes in the matter of taste, our servant, Sarah, on seeing them, evinced no sign of pleasure, but merely said 'she thought they looked very well as they was before'.

APRIL 26. Got some more red enamel paint (red, to my mind, being the best colour), and painted the coal-scuttle, and the backs of our *Shakespeare*, the binding of which had almost worn out.

APRIL 27. Painted the bath red, and was delighted with the result. Sorry to say Carrie was not, in fact we had a few words about it. She said I ought to have consulted her, and she had never heard of such a thing as a bath being painted red. I replied: 'It's merely a matter of taste.'

APRIL 29, SUNDAY. Woke up with a fearful headache and strong symptoms of a cold. Carrie, with a perversity which is just like her, said it was 'painter's colic', and was the result of my having spent the last few days with my nose over a paint-pot. I told her firmly that I knew a great deal better what was the matter with me than she did. I had got a chill, and decided to have a bath as hot as I could bear it. Bath ready – could scarcely bear it so hot. I persevered, and got in; very hot, but very acceptable. I lay still for some time. On moving my hand above the surface of the water, I experienced the greatest fright I ever received in the whole course of my life; for imagine my horror on discovering my hand, as I thought, full of blood. My first thought was that I had ruptured an artery, and was bleeding to death, and should be dis-covered, later on, looking like a second Marat, as I remember seeing him in Madame Tussaud's. My second thought was to ring the bell, but remem-bered there was no bell to ring. My third was, that there was nothing but the enamel paint, which had dissolved with boiling water. I stepped out of the bath, perfectly red all over, resembling the Red Indians I have seen depicted at an East-End theatre. I determined not to say a word to Carrie, but to tell Farmerson to come on Monday and paint the bath white.

George and Weedon Grossmith
THE DIARY OF A NOBODY *1892*

The combination of warmth and smooth porcelain often tempted a most unwelcome visitor to call:

> I have fought a grizzly bear,
> Tracked a cobra to its lair,
> Killed a crocodile who dared to cross my path;
> But the thing I really dread
> When I've just got out of bed
> Is to find that there's a spider in the bath.
>
> I've no fear of wasps or bees,
> Mosquitoes only tease,

I rather like a cricket on the hearth;
But my blood runs cold to meet
In pyjamas and bare feet
With a great big hairy spider in the bath.

I have faced a charging bull in Barcelona,
I have dragged a mountain lioness from her cub,
I've restored a mad gorilla to its owner
But I don't dare to face that Tub...

What a frightful-looking beast –
Half an inch across at least –
It would frighten even Superman or Garth,
There's contempt it can't disguise
In the little beady eyes
Of the spider sitting glowering in the bath.

It ignores my every lunge
With the back-brush and the sponge;
I have bombed it with 'A Present from Penarth';
But it doesn't mind at all –
It just rolls into a ball
And simply goes on squatting in the bath...

For hours we have been locked in endless struggle;
I have lured it to the deep end, by the drain;
At last I think I've washed it down the plug-'ole
But here it comes a-crawling up the chain!

Now it's time for me to shave
Though my nerves will not behave,
And there's bound to be a fearful aftermath;
So before I cut my throat
I shall leave this final note:
DRIVEN TO IT –
    BY THE SPIDER IN THE BATH!

Michael Flanders and Donald Swann
THE SONGS OF MICHAEL FLANDERS AND DONALD SWANN

It seems that a huge percentage of all accidents occur in the home, so it is perhaps not surprising that the bathroom, the centre of family activity at least twice a day, has its share of jeopardies. The British Bathroom has been the stage for many a deeply harrowing drama:

The pub. Pub hubbub, over which:

LANDLORD: (*shouting*) Time, gentlemen, please! All your glasses please, gents. Come on, Mr. Glum, please let me get finished up early tonight. It's my bath-night, Mr. Glum, and you know how much I love a good old soak.

MR. GLUM: Yes, I've met her. But don't you talk to me about bath-nights, Ted. Not after what happened to *me* last week. Cor! That was something I shall remember till the day I die – if I'm spared that long. What happened was – (*changing to gently chiding tone*) – Ah, Ted, you weren't about to pour yet *another* brown ale in this glass, were you?

LANDLORD: No I wasn't, Mr. Glum.

MR. GLUM: (*grimly*) I thought you weren't! So shove one in there. No, reverting to last week, what happened was, I'd gone up to have a bath at my usual time – first of the month – and downstairs I'd left my son Ron – you know my boy Ron, don't you?

LANDLORD: He the one with the Tommy Steele haircut?

MR. GLUM: That's him. Except it's not a Tommy Steele haircut, it's a Davy Crockett hat gone mangy. Anyway, while I'm upstairs, he's on the sofa in our front room with his fiancée, Eth. And what *transpired* – as it transpires . . .

Music. The Glums' sitting-room,

ETH: Oh, Ron... Your father started having his bath at seven – it's now gone ten and he's still up there! That can't be good for an old man. Why should he be in that bath for three hours?

RON: Perhaps he's a *dirty* old man.

ETH: Even so, no one should stay in there all that time. I mean, I like my bath, but even allowing for a good old wallow – I'm in and out in twenty minutes. Oh, wouldn't you like to just pop your head round the bathroom door?

RON: (*eagerly*) Oh yes, Eth.

ETH: Your *father's* door! Please, Ron, please pop up and make sure nothing's happened to him.

RON: I'd rather not, Eth. I already popped up once – just after he got into the bath. He threw the dirty linen at me.

ETH: Whyever for?

RON: (*resentful*) Just 'cos I put Barbara Kelly in there with him.

ETH: Barbara Kelly?

RON: My goldfish. Poor little thing's got to stretch her fins somewhere.

ETH: But that's even more worrying, Ron. If Mr. Glum got into one of his *rages*...! A heavily built man like him all worked-up in a steamy little bathroom ...! Ron, he could go out just like *that*!

RON: Oh no, he couldn't go out like that, Eth. He'd be arrested.

ETH: What I meant, Ron –

RON: (*firmly*) Look, Eth, you're just making a mountain out of a mole-hole. Dad's all right. If anything had happened to him, we'd have heard.

From upstairs comes a muffled shout of infuriated frustration . . .

ETH: Ron, isn't that him? Listen.

From upstairs, more unintelligible shouting. This time, a muffled tirade of baffled profanity.

RON: (*triumphant*) There, Eth. See? (*fondly*) He's singing!

ETH: That was no singing, Ron, He's in difficulties! (*Shout*) Mr. Glum, are you feeling all right?

The bathroom. Mr. Glum is in the bath.

MR. GLUM: (*furious shout*) All right? No, I'm not all right. I can't get meself out of the *bath*!

Music and back to the pub.   *Pub hubbub.*

LANDLORD: Well, strike me rotten! Got your big toe jammed in the plug-hole? Dear oh dear. Must have been a bit unpleasant, I should think.

MR. GLUM: (*heavy sarcasm*) Oh no, Ted, it was delightful. If there's one thing I can thoroughly recommend, it's sitting for three hours in rapidly cooling water, with your toe stuck in the waste-pipe, and a flipping goldfish sporting round your southern hemisphere.

LANDLORD: Still you were lucky your Ron and Eth were there to lend a hand. Come to think of it, though, Eth couldn't have been that much help, really. Not in the circumstances.

MR. GLUM: Well, as it happens, we got *round* that

particular difficulty. I told Ron to empty a few packets of gravy browning into the bath water.

LANDLORD: Gravy browning...? Oh, that was shrewd, Mr. Glum. That really was shrewd.

MR. GLUM: Shrewd enough for *you* to think about pouring some brown in? (*As landlord pours –*) Yes, it worked a treat. By the time Ron had emptied the twelfth packet in, I'd have got a 'U' Certificate from any Watch Committee in the country. 'Course he had to stir it *round* a little...

Music and we're back in the bathroom.

MR. GLUM: That's it, Ron, give it a good swish round. Want to try one more packet for luck?

Knock on door.

ETH: (*Off*) All right for me to come in yet, Mr. Glum?

MR. GLUM: Hang on, Eth! How's it seem to *you*, Ron?

RON: Just a minute, Dad.

Ron licks his lips.

RON: Lovely.

MR. GLUM: I didn't mean *taste* it! Oh, it seems dark enough now. (*Calls*) Right ho, Eth, I'm decent.

The door opens and Eth enters.

ETH: Hallo, Mr. Glum.

MR. GLUM: (*weak voice*) Hallo, my dear. You'll pardon me not getting up. Well, Eth, this is a fine predicament for a man of my years to find himself in, eh? Sitting here like The Browning Version.

59

ETH: It's too awful, Mr. Glum. But what did you want to put your big toe in the plug-hole for in the first place?

MR. GLUM: (*irritable*) I didn't *want* to put it in. I had to put it in! There wasn't no plug.

ETH: No plug?

MR. GLUM: This afternoon, my son – your husband-to-be – he went round and collected the plug from the bath, the plug from the basin, the plug from the kitchen sink, both knobs off the telly and the check lino out the scullery.

ETH: Ron – whatever for?

RON: I'm teaching myself to play draughts.

MR. GLUM: Consequence was, when I turned on the tap this evening – what happened? The water runs straight out.

ETH: Yes, it would, wouldn't it?

MR. GLUM: Never mind it would, wouldn't it, it did, didn't it? The only thing I could do was get undressed, place myself in the *empty* bath and this time, prior to turning the taps on, stuff me big toe down the plug-hole. That part alone gave me a severe emotional shock.

ETH: Emotional shock?

MR. GLUM: You try sitting down naked on cold porcelain! But at least the bath filled up all right, so – after passing a lightly soaped flannel over my salient features, I lay me head back in the water, did my walrus impersonation – then went to get *out*. And what did I find? That toe was stuck fast! Wedged like a bung in a beer-barrel! Nothing'll shift it!

ETH: And that's how you've been for three hours? Oh, Ron, he hasn't even had any supper. Shouldn't you bring him up some?

RON: I think that might make him feel worse, Eth.

ETH: Why, Ron?

RON: It was toad in the hole.

MR. GLUM: Cor lummy, it's like Fate itself is perspiring against me.

ETH: Now, try not to get embittered, Mr. Glum. There must be *some* way of – look, how about this. Suppose we put a broomstick under your knee, wedge it against the side of the bath, then Ron and I throw all our weight on the other end. What would happen?

MR. GLUM: You'd break my ruddy *leg*, that's what would happen! Do you think I haven't been cudgelling my brains for a way out? There isn't one. I tell you, Ethel, I won't be shifted from this bathroom without major surgery! All because my dear son took it into his head to – (*emits a sudden, surprisingly maidenly shriek.*)

ETH: What is it?

MR. GLUM: That rotten *goldfish*! Keeps doing that when I least *expect* it. Where is it? (*Grabbing about in the dark water*) Just let me get my hands on it. I'll teach it to treat me like a subterranean grotto! (*Paddles his hand round.*)

RON: Watch it, Dad. You thrash around like that, you'll thin your gravy.

MR. GLUM: It's all so inexplicable. If the perishing toe went in, why won't it come out?

ETH: Oh, that's quite easily explainable, Mr. Glum. It was the heat of the hot water.

61

MR. GLUM: Eh?

ETH: It made your big toe swell. You see, heat always makes things get bigger.

RON: She's quite right, Dad. That's why days are longer in the summer than they are in the winter.

MR. GLUM: Thank you very much. So your suggestion is that I sit here till the winter?

ETH: Oh no, Mr. Glum. But we're on the right track.

MR. GLUM: How d'you mean?

ETH: Well, if we could – Ron, can you think of some way for your father to cool his big toe down?

RON: I think so, Eth.

MR. GLUM: How, Ron?

RON: Well, it seems obvious to me, Dad.

MR. GLUM: All right, don't keep it a secret. How can I cool that toe down?

RON: Take it out and blow on it.

MR. GLUM: (*containing his feelings*) Take it out and . . . Ron?

RON: Yes, Dad?

MR. GLUM: Once and for all, *admit* something to me. I just want the satisfaction of hearing you admit it.

RON: What, Dad?

MR. GLUM: Sometimes you're as dim as a sweep's ear-'ole! Aren't you?

RON: Yes, Dad.

MR. GLUM: Not just 'Yes, Dad'. Admit it.

RON: Sometimes I'm as dim as a sweep's ear-'ole.

MR. GLUM: Just plain honest-to-goodness gormless.

RON: Just plain honest-to-goodness gormless.

MR. GLUM: And stupid *with* it.

RON: And stupid *with* it.

MR. GLUM: Thank you, Ron. At least, that's made me feel a *little* better.

RON: I tell you one thing about me though, Dad.

MR. GLUM: What's that?

RON: I've never got my big toe stuck in a plughole.

MR. GLUM: *(to Eth, wildly)* Either take him away or – ! Look at me flesh – it's started going all *crinkly*. What with that and the gravy, I'll be like the edge of a steak-and-kidney pie. Please, Eth – think!

ETH: We are thinking, Mr. Glum. You really mustn't be so impatient.

MR. GLUM: Impatient? For heaven's sake, what am I asking? If they can raise ninety thousand tons of shipping out the Suez Canal, surely you two can get one old man's toe out a waste-pipe.

ETH: Waste-pipe! Yes, of course – that is a *pipe*, isn't it! I'd forgotten that. Ron – why don't we tackle the problem the other way about?

RON: You mean push his *head* in?

ETH: No, Ron. Get at the toe from the other end of the waste-pipe!

MR. GLUM: Ah! Now that's the first sensible suggestion yet. Yes – 'stead of *pulling* at the toe, get to a position where you can *push* at it from beneath. Ron –

RON: Yes, Dad?

MR. GLUM: Bend down and have a look at the bottom of the bath.

Effect. Bubbling.

MR. GLUM: Trouble is, you see, Eth – his mind has never really caught up with his body.

ETH: Mr. Glum, he'll drown!

Ron comes out of the water, gasping and spluttering.

RON: (*breathing hard*) Couldn't see *anything*, Dad. There was a toe in the way.

MR. GLUM: And the moment I get back the use of that toe, I know exactly where I'm going to place it. (*Patiently*) Ron, look *underneath* the bath. Down under the plug-hole. What you should find there is a waste-pipe coming out and forming a 'U'.

RON: A 'U'.

MR. GLUM: A 'U'. And at the base of that 'U' there is a nut.

RON: A nut.

MR. GLUM: A nut. Or, if you prefer – 'U' again. Now if you go and *undo* that nut, you will perceive a *hole* which, if you shove something up it, you can easily reach my ill-fated toe. Do you understand?

MR. GLUM AND RON: (*pause; then, together*) No, Dad.

ETH: I've got it, Ron. And it unscrews quite . . . (*grunt*) . . . Ah!   And there's the hole – oh, it can only be a couple of inches from the end of Mr.

Glum's toe.   Quick, Ron, get something out the bathroom cabinet you can shove up and push with.

RON: Right ho, Eth.

ETH: This'll do it, Mr. Glum. You're only a few seconds away from freedom now. See where you've got to push up, Ron?

RON: I see, Eth. Ready, Dad?

MR. GLUM: I been ready for three hours. A good hard push now, son.

RON: Right ho, Dad. (*Grunt of effort.*)

MR. GLUM: (*howl of agony*) Aagh! What did you –?

RON: You said find something to –

MR. GLUM: Not scissors! You great brainless –! That hole's only a couple of *inches* from where my toe is. You should be able to push it out with your finger.

RON: My finger. Ah! Question is . . . No, I've got a taller one somewhere. Ah, thought so. Stand by, Dad.

MR. GLUM: Feel me toe?

RON: Just a mo', just a mo' . . . Ah! Contact!

MR. GLUM: (*excited*) Now *push*, lad. *Hard*! All your weight behind it. I can feel it moving, moving – one more ought to . . . (*Triumph*) Aah! (*His foot pops out of water.*) I'm free! Free! Oh, the relief, the – Eth, I can't thank you enough for – (*his voice breaks.*)

ETH: Oh, that's all right.

MR. GLUM: And Ron – them remarks I made about you being dim and gormless and stupid . . . well, I apologize, son. It was just the heat of the moment. Will you – will you shake hands and say you forgive your nasty-tempered old Daddy?

RON: No, I won't, Dad.

MR. GLUM: Oh, no, Ron, don't bear grudges. Come on, stand up and shake hands.

RON: I just can't, Dad.

MR. GLUM: What do you mean 'can't'?

RON: It's my finger. Look – It seems to be stuck in the hole where...

MR. GLUM: Oh, gawd no! Oh, you dim, gormless, stupid, no-good –

BRING UP MUSIC AND FADE

Frank Muir and Denis Norden
From the radio programme TAKE IT FROM HERE, 1959

We leave the subject of baths as we began, with the musings of a writer immersed in his bath's comforting warmth.

But this time the writer is a little *triste*. He has noticed his toes and broods upon their loss of status:

> In the tub we soak our skin
> and drowse and meditate within.
>
> The mirror clouds, the vapors rise,
> We view our toes with sad surprise;
>
> The toes that mother kissed and counted,
> The since neglected and unwanted.

Edward Newman Horn (*1903?–1976*)

Next to the bath stands the washbasin. In a little hollow on its top there is a sliver of soap the size and thickness of an oval

66

postage stamp (how does a new cake of soap manage to reduce itself overnight to a barely visible sliver, which then lasts for three weeks?). There is also a pair of toothbrushes, colour-coded blue and pink, and a tube of toothpaste which has lost its cap.

Although in the past soap was mainly used for scrubbing and doing the laundry there was enough demand for it in Tudor times to support a Soapmakers' Guild, and Charles II farmed out the monopoly rights to manufacture it for a huge sum. The best soap, that is to say the slightly milder kind which did not immediately cause the user's skin to go scarlet and peel off, was imported from Castile in Spain.

But most households of any size boiled up their own. It was one of those domestic duties which fell to the womenfolk, like moulding the candles, brewing the beer, and preparing the medicines, cosmetics and herbal cure-alls which are sold nowadays under the horrid title of 'assorted toiletries'.

For those readers whose ambition to achieve self-sufficiency extends to assorted toiletries I give details of some old recipes. It is only fair to point out that when ordering some of the ingredients, e.g. dragon's-blood, japan-earth, virgin's wax, it might be as well to give your local chemist a few days' notice:

How to make Ball Soap; of great Use in Families.

THIS soap is easily made, and goes much farther than any of the other soaps. You are to make a lee from ashes and tallow; then put the lees into a copper, and boil them till the watery part is quite gone, and there remains nothing in the copper but a sort of nitrous matter (the very strength and essence of the lee) to this the tallow is put, and the copper kept boiling and stirring for above half an hour, in which time the soap is made; it is then taken out of the copper, and put into tubs, or baskets, with sheets in them, and immediately (whilst warm) made into balls. You are to take notice, that it requires near 24 hours to boil away the watery part of the lee.

Peregrine Montague, Gent. (*mid-18th. century*)
THE FAMILY POCKET-BOOK
or, FOUNTAIN OF TRUE AND USEFUL KNOWLEDGE,
COMPILED AFTER THIRTY YEARS EXPERIENCE.

Factory-made toothbrushes are a product of our modern world and when they first appeared seemed a needless extravagance:

Toothbrushes were not in general use; few
could afford to buy such luxuries; but the women
took a pride in their strong white teeth and cleaned
them with a scrap of clean wet rag dipped in salt.
Some of the men used soot as a sort of tooth-
powder.

Flora Thompson.
LARK RISE TO CANDLEFORD.

Other tooth-powder substitutes used down the centuries besides soot, salt and perfumed water were pumicestone and – in Spain, according to Erasmus – human urine. Or you could put together a mixture of your own from one of the tried and true recipes published:

How to make the King of France's Teeth Powder, famous for making the Teeth white, and preserving them from the Scurvy.

Take of chalk and pebble-stones burnt, of each one oz. myrrh, bole-armoniac and dragon's-blood, of each half an ounce, of ammoniacum and cuttle-bones, of each 3 drachms, let them be all finely powder'd.

THE FAMILY INSTRUCTOR OF THE KNOWLEDGE OF MEDICINE. c. 1760.

Bad teeth were commonplace. Queen Elizabeth I had troublesome teeth; discoloured and green to begin with and finally, as gleefully reported back by foreign diplomats, virtually black, and there were recipes for keeping teeth steady and painless:

To fasten loose Teeth, and prevent the Tooth-ach.

Take myrrh and japan-earth, of each two drachms; bruise and boil them in a pint of claret, to the consumption of the third part, then strain it, and let it settle, wash your mouth with the clearest every morning. If your teeth are very foul, take a rag, and dip it in spirits of vitriol, and rub your teeth with it, washing your mouth with water after it.

Ibid.

The hint for cleaning foul teeth must have been effective as vitriol is used nowadays for cleaning badly stained baths.

A favoured form of primitive toothbrush was the end of a twig (hazel was favourite) but this ancient practice worried an eighteenth century gentleman who recommended that nothing more rigid than a sponge should be employed:

I hope you take great care of your mouth and teeth, and that you clean them well every morning with a ſpunge and tepid water, with a few drops of arquebuſade water dropped into it; beſides waſhing your mouth carefully after every meal. I do inſiſt upon your never uſing thoſe ſticks, or any hard ſubſtance whatſoever, which always rub away the gums, and deſtroy the varniſh of the teeth. I ſpeak this from woeful experience; for my negligence of my teeth, when I was younger than you are, made them bad; and afterwards, my deſire to have them look better, made me uſe ſticks, irons, &c. which totally deſtroyed them; ſo that I have not now above ſix or ſeven left. I loſt one this morning, which ſuggeſted this advice to you.

Lord Chesterfield's Letters to his son.
Letter LXXXV. London, 15 February, 1754.

'Arquebusade' was a lotion much valued for staunching gunshot wounds.

The great medical school of Salernum took the view that toothache was caused by small worms burrowing into the tooth and setting up home there and that the cure was to smoke them out:

If in your teeth you hap to be tormented,
This means some little worms therein do breed:
Which pain (if heed be taken) may be prevented,
By keeping clean your teeth when as you feed.
Burn Frankincense (a gum not evil scented)
Put Henbane into this, and Onion seed,
And in a Tunnel to the Tooth that's hollow,
Convey the smoke thereof, and ease shall follow.

REGIMEN SANITATIS SALERNITANUM
English version by Sir John Harington, 1609

The science of dental care had made slow progress since Salernum. When the tooth had rotted irrevocably it had to be pulled out; a job for the barber or for a powerfully-shouldered quack at a Fair. But by the end of the eighteenth century a lot more was known about what caused teeth to go bad. And teeth became important enough to have a branch of medicine devoted to their study and care – dentistry:

> Whene'er along the ivory disks are seen
> The rapid traces of the dark gangrene,
> When caries comes, with stealthy pace, to throw
> Corrosive ink-spots on those banks of snow,
> Brook no delay, ye trembling, suffering Fair
> But fly for refuge to the Dentist's care.

Solyman Brown (1790–1865?)
THE DENTIAD

Up to the nineteenth century it was a widely held view in the Western world that washing the hair was an act of eccentricity and very dangerous to bodily health.

It took a poet of great courage (he personally founded Newfoundland) to advocate a washing of the head not just once a year but *quarterly*:

> *Is bathing of the head wholesome?*
> You shall find it wonderful expedient if you bathe
> your head four times in the year, and that with hot
> lye made of ashes. After which you must cause one
> presently to pour two or three gallons of cold
> fountain water upon your head. Then let your
> head be dried with cold towels. Which sudden
> pouring down of cold water, although it doth
> mightily terrify you, yet nevertheless it is very
> good, for thereby the natural heat is stirred within
> the body, baldness is kept back, and the memory
> is quickened.

William Vaughan (1557–1641)
NATURALL AND ARTIFICIAL DIRECTIONS FOR HEALTH

The poet also recommended eating young ducks which had been stifled in borage smoke to 'increase natural seed'.

More typical was an eighteenth century reaction to a recipe for an oatmeal-and-egg shampoo:

> The Method is this, Let a Woman wash her Hair with a Mixture of beaten Eggs and Oatmeal, and go afterwards into a warm Bath, and she will poison the Water to such a Degree, that there will be a stinking noisome Smell communicated to it, and a great Quantity of a light and frothy Sea Green Matter will swim in it; the whole Body of the Water will also partake of this Colour, and it will taint the very Walls, tinging them green and making them stink.

'Sir' John Hill (*1716?–1775*)
A REVIEW OF THE ROYAL SOCIETY

Most of the recipes which our fore-parents used for their cosmetics were cheerfully medieval, relying heavily on blind trust in mumbo-jumbo and the belief that something with a long name must be beneficial:

> To clere, to clense, and to mundifie the face use stufes and bathes, and euery mornyne after keymyng of the head, wype the face with a Skarlet cloth, and washe not the face ofte, but ones a weke anoynt the face a lytle ouer with the oyle of Costine, and vse to eat *Electuary de aromatibus*, or the confection of Anacardine, or the syrupe of Fumitery, or confection of Manna . . .

Andrew Boorde (*1490?–1549*)
BREUYARY OF HEALTH

The head anointed with the juice of leeks preserveth the hair from falling. A mouse roasted and given to children to eat remedieth pissing the bed.

THE WIDDOWES TREASURE 1595

To preserve the Face from being deform'd by the Small-pox.

Take an ounce and a half of pomatum; of oil of almonds one ounce; of spermaceti and virgin's wax, of each three drachms; of damask rose-water one ounce, set them all together over the fire, and as soon as they are melted take them off, let them stand then till they are cold, then make a hole, and drain out the water, and with a feather anoint the patient's face.

THE FAMILY INSTRUCTOR IN THE KNOWLEDGE OF MEDICINE C. 1760

One of the remedies makes one feel that one would prefer to keep the sore lip, unsightly though it might be:

For a Bruise, occasion'd by a Cold.

Take horse-dung and sheep's suet, of each equal parts, boil them well together, and apply warm to the part affected, like a poultice.

Ibid.

Our last recipe seems to require the user to slap on a mixture of calvesfoot-jelly and bread-and-butter pudding:

A Very Good Water to Make the Face Appear of the Age of 25 year

Take a couple of calves' feet and seethe them in seven pound of river water until half be consumed; then put in a pound of rice, and let it seethe with crumbs of fine manchet bread steeped in milk, two pounds of fresh butter and seven new laid eggs with their shells and all: set those all things to distil, and into the water that shall come of it out a little camphor and saccharine alum, and you shall have an excellent noble thing of it.

THE SECRETS OF THE REVEREND MAISTER ALEXIS OF PIEMINT 1558
trans.: William Warde

Bizarre and revolting though most of the early cures appear to modern eyes it is reasonable to suppose that some of them must have done *some* good because they appeared over a period of many centuries and were reprinted endlessly. Take a scientifically-minded gentleman's recipe for eye-lotion:

Take *Paracelsus's Zebethum Occidentale*, (*viz.* Human Dung) of a good Colour and Consistence, dry it slowly till it be pulverable: Then reduce it into an impalpable Powder; which is to be blown once, twice or thrice a Day, as occasion shall require, into the Patient's Eyes.

The Hon. Robert Boyle (*1627–1691*)
MEDICINAL EXPERIMENTS

This was the Boyle who propounded 'Boyle's Law'.

In previous centuries a household's medical and cosmetic needs required a large room to themselves. Herbs had to be hung to dry; pestles and mortars, jars and bottles, drying cabinets, scales, tubs of ingredients, all had to be stored, and a fair amount of space had to be allocated to the various vigorous processes which were necessary, e.g., distillation, seething, beating, grinding, pulverizing.

Nowadays our remedies are prepared for us, and they come in pleasant little bottles which we can arrange neatly in a box on the wall specially designed for our modern bathrooms – the Medicine Cabinet:

> I am sure that many a husband has wanted to wrench the family medicine cabinet off the wall and throw it out of the window, if only because the average medicine cabinet is so filled with mysterious bottles and unidentifiable objects of all kinds that it is a source of constant bewilderment and exasperation to the American male. Surely the British medicine cabinet and the French medicine cabinet and all the other medicine cabinets must be simpler and better ordered than ours. It may be that the American habit of saving everything and never throwing anything away, even empty bottles, causes the domestic medicine cabinet to become as cluttered in its small way as the American attic becomes cluttered in a major way. I have encountered few medicine cabinets in this country which were not pack-jammed with something between a hundred and fifty and two hundred different items, from dental floss to boracic acid, from razor blades to sodium perborate, from adhesive tape to coconut oil. Even the neatest wife will put off clearing out the medicine cabinet on the ground that she has something else to do that is more important at the moment, or more diverting. It was in the apartment of such a wife and her husband that I became enormously involved with a medicine cabinet one morning not long ago.

I had spent the week-end with this couple – they live on East Tenth Street near Fifth Avenue – such a week-end as left me reluctant to rise up on Monday morning with bright and shining face and go to work. They got up and went to work, but I didn't. I didn't get up until about two-thirty in the afternoon. I had my face all lathered for shaving and the wash-bowl was full of hot water when suddenly I cut myself with the razor. I cut my ear. Very few men cut their ears with razors, but I do, possibly because I was taught the old Spencerian free-wrist movement by my writing teacher in the grammar grades. The ear bleeds rather profusely when cut with a razor and is difficult to get at. More angry than hurt, I jerked open the door of the medicine cabinet to see if I could see a styptic pencil, and out fell, from the top shelf, a little black paper packet containing nine needles. It seems that this wife kept a little packet containing nine needles on the top shelf of the medicine cabinet. The packet fell into the soapy water of the wash-bowl, where the paper rapidly disintegrated, leaving nine needles at large in the bowl. I was, naturally enough, not in the best condition, either physical or mental, to recover nine needles from a wash-bowl. No gentleman who has lather on his face and whose ear is bleeding is in the best condition for anything, even something involving the handling of nine large blunt objects.

It did not seem wise to me to pull the plug out of the wash-bowl and let the needles go down the drain. I had visions of clogging up the plumbing system of the house, and also a vague fear of causing short circuits somehow or other (I know very little about electricity and I don't want to have it explained to me). Finally I groped very gently around the bowl and eventually had four of the needles in the palm of one hand and three in the palm of the other – two I couldn't find. If I thought quickly and clearly I wouldn't have done that. A lathered man whose ear is bleeding and who has four wet needles in one hand and three in the other may be said to have reached the lowest known point of human efficiency. There is nothing he can do but stand there. I tried transferring the needles in my left hand to the palm of my right hand, but I couldn't get them off my left hand. Wet needles cling to you. In the end I wiped the needles off on to a bath-towel which was hanging on a rod above the bath-tub. It was the only towel that I could find. I had to dry my hands afterwards on the bath-mat. Then I tried to find the needles in the towel. Hunting for seven needles in a bath-towel is the most tedious occupation I have ever engaged in. I could find only five of them. With the two that had been left in the bowl, that meant there were four needles in all missing – two in the wash-bowl and two others lurking in the towel or lying in the bath-tub under the towel. Frightful thoughts came to me of what might happen to anyone who used that towel or washed his face in the bowl or got into the tub, if I didn't find the missing needles. Well, I didn't find them. I sat down on the edge of the tub to think, and I decided finally that the only thing to do was wrap up the towel in a newspaper and take it away with me. I also decided to leave a note for my friends explaining as clearly as I could that I was afraid there were two needles in the bath-tub and two needles in the wash-bowl, and that they better be careful.

I looked everywhere in the apartment, but I could not find a pencil, or a pen, or a typewriter. I could find pieces of paper, but nothing with which to write on them. I don't know what gave me the idea – a movie I had seen, perhaps, or a story I had read – but I suddenly thought of writing a message with a lipstick. The wife might have an extra lipstick lying around and, if so, I concluded it would be in the medicine cabinet. I went back to the medicine cabinet and began poking around in it for a lipstick. I saw what I thought looked like the metal tip of one, and I got two fingers around it and began to pull gently – it was under a lot of things. Every object in the medicine cabinet began to slide. Bottles broke in the wash-bowl and on the floor; red, brown, and white liquids spurted; nail files, scissors, razor blades, and miscellaneous objects sang and clattered and tinkled. I was covered with perfume, peroxide, and cold cream.

It took me half an hour to get the debris all together in the middle of the bathroom floor. I made no attempt to put anything back in the medicine cabinet. I knew it would take a steadier hand than mine and a less shattered spirit. Before I went away (only partly shaved) and abandoned the shambles, I left a note saying that I was afraid there were needles in the bath-tub and the wash-bowl and that I had taken their towel and that I would call up and tell them everything – I wrote it in iodine with the end of a toothbrush. I have not called up yet, I am sorry to say. I have neither found the courage nor thought up the words to explain what happened. I suppose my friends believe that I deliberately smashed up their bathroom and stole their towel. I don't know for sure, because they have not yet called me up, either.

James Thurber (*1894–1961*)
NINE NEEDLES

'Toilet paper' – as it is described in the trade – is a modern invention dating back only as far as the 1880s, when it became available from the British Perforated Paper Company; an excellent example of a go-ahead company creating public demand for a product for which there was no need.

Our ancestors would have laughed themselves silly at the notion of us paying good money to buy rolls of plain paper when our houses are full of old magazines and newsprint.

In ancient times, before the invention of paper, the cleaning-off problem was solved in a number of ways. Water was the answer where water existed. Failing that it was a matter of using a scraper or an abrasive.

The Romans favoured a kind of miniature hockey-stick (in wood or precious metal according to the user's status), or a sponge on the end of a stick (origin of the phrase 'to get hold of the wrong end of the stick'?).

In desert areas it was normal to use sand, powdered brick, or earth. A book on Muslim law published as late as 1882, *Manuel de Jurisprudence Musulman selon le Rite de Chafi*, recommends using stones: 'There shall be three stones employed or three sides of the same stone'.

A favourite scraper throughout the ages, probably because of its convenient shape and easy availability, was a mussel shell. A writer in the eighteenth century recalls a charming incident involving its use:

'Whereas I have known an old woman in Holland set herself on the next hole to a gentleman, and civilly offer him her muscle shell by way of scraper after she had done with it herself.'

PHILOSOPHICAL DIALOGUE CONCERNING DECENCY 1751

Perhaps a similar encounter in a two-seater inspired the poet to write:

Then her cheek was pale and thinner than should
    be for one so young,
And her eye on all my motions with a mute
    observance hung.

Alfred Lord Tennyson (*1809–1892*)
LOCKSLEY HALL

A form of scraper which lingered on and perhaps is still in use in rural America is the corncob, a box of which would be to hand in all well-appointed privies:

> 'Now, about her furnishin's. I can give you a nail
> or hook for the catalogue, and besides, a box for
> cobs. You take your pa, for instance; he's of the old
> school and naturally he'd prefer the box; so put
> 'em both in, Elmer.

Charles Sale
THE SPECIALIST. 1930

Charles (Chick) Sale's tiny best-seller, *The Specialist*, is a publishing phenomenon. Sale was not an author or a journalist but a character comedian whose best-known act was to play the part of an old craftsman, Lem Putt, whose speciality, and love, was building privies. Piracy and plagiarism was a great problem to comedians in the early years of this century and Sale was persuaded to establish his copyright on the character by putting him into print. In 1929 he set up a little publishing company for the sole purpose of printing *The Specialist*.

It has never since been out of print. Its sales exceed a million, in ten languages. It is thirty pages long and has about 3000 words. George Bernard Shaw wrote – on one of his famous postcards – 'The illustrations are excellent; but the frontispiece fails in courage. Clearly it should represent the Elmer family *in situ*. G.B.S.'

A rural American privy in the heat of summer, cool beneath a leafy tree, a box of soft, fresh cobs waiting, sounds tolerable enough. However, the seasons changed. And some parents practised thrift:

> But when the crust was on the snow and the sullen
> skies were gray,
> In sooth the building was no place where one could
> wish to stay.
> We did our duties promptly, there one purpose
> swayed the mind;

We tarried not, nor lingered long on what we left
    behind.
The torture of that icy seat would make a Spartan
    sob,
For needs must scrape the goose flesh with a
    lacerating cob,
That from a frost-encrusted nail, was suspended
    by a string –
For Father was a frugal man and wasted not a
    thing.

James Whitcomb Riley (*1849–1916*)
THE OLD BACKHOUSE

A soft alternative to those of tender skin who had to ply the mussel shell or lacerating cob came in the late fifteenth century when the development of printing brought about a massive increase in the manufacture of paper. From the days of Queen Elizabeth I it became the custom to retire to stool with a book, ripping out pages as they were called for.

This use to which their work was put did not please authors. Robert Herrick wrote a little cautionary verse in his book to give it protection:

Who with thy leaves shall wipe (at need)
The place, where swelling *Piles* do breed:
May every ill, that bites, or smarts,
Perplex him in his hinder-parts.

Robert Herrick (*1591–1674*)
TO HIS BOOKE

Correspondence also came in handy:

> I am seated in the necessary house. I have your
> letter before me. Soon it will be behind me.

Anon.

By the eighteenth century the use of books in the privy was so commonplace that a poem was published with the title:

BUM-FODDER
for the
LADIES
a
POEM
(Upon Soft PAPER)
1753

The poem itself turned out to be a deeply boring political satire. 'Bum-fodder' is, of course, the origin of the modern word 'bumph'.

The good point about taking a book into the privy with you was that the time spent in there was not wasted but spent on self-improvement.

Samuel Johnson, musing on the fact that as flogging decreased in the great schools so did learning, commented 'What the boys get at one end they lose at the other.' One could say about someone sitting in the privy reading and tearing out pages 'What they lose at one end they gain at the other.'

Reading and tearing out the pages was highly recommended by many eminent men, including Lord Chesterfield, who wrote to his son:

I knew a gentleman, who was fo good a manager of his time, that he would not even lofe that fmall portion of it, which the calls of nature obliged him to pafs in the neceffary-houfe ; but gradually went through all the Latin Poets, in thofe moments. He bought, for example, a common edition of Horace, of which he tore off gradually a couple of pages, carried them with him to that neceffary place, read them firft, and then fent them down as a facrifice to Cloacina : this was fo much time fairly gained ; and I recommend to you to follow his example. It is better than only doing what you cannot help doing at thofe moments; and it will make any book, which you fhall read in that manner, very prefent in your mind. Books of fcience, and of a grave fort, muft be read with continuity; but there are very many, and even very ufeful ones, which may be read with advantage by fnatches, and unconnectedly; fuch are all the good Latin poets, except Virgil in his Æneid: and fuch are moft of the modern poets, in which you will find many pieces worth reading, that will not take up above feven or eight minutes. Bayle's, Moreri's, and other dictionaries, are proper books to take and fhut up for the little intervals of (otherwife) idle time, that every body has in the courfe of the day, between either their ftudies or their pleafures. Good night.

Lord Chesterfield. Letters to his Son.
Letter Cl, London, December the 11th. O.S. 1747.

The noble Lord Chesterfield would hardly have been pleased had he known that his advice was to be encapsulated for all time in a humble limerick:

> There was a young fellow named Chivy
> Who, whenever he went to the privy,
> First solaced his mind,
> Then wiped his behind,
> With some well-chosen pages of Livy.

Anon.
QUOTED IN THE LIMERICK ed.: G. Legman

Books are rarely torn up for lavatorial purposes these days; they are too valuable and there are many cheaper sources of waste paper. But they are still read there (John Cowper Powys revealed that he had read his way, seated, through *The Anatomy of Melancholy*, *Tristram Shandy*, half of *Don Quixote*, all of Rabelais and two volumes of the works of Montaigne). Further evidence came in *The Bookseller* of Dec. 19 and 26, 1981 which reported that Crown Paint's Gallup survey into what people would choose to have as 'fantasy extras' in their 'dream loo' produced the following list:

1. A musical toilet-paper holder.
2. Gold taps.
3. Built-in stereo.
4. A heated seat.
5. A copy of *Jane's Fighting Ships*.

One of the traditional American sources of suitable paper in farming areas was the enormously thick mail-order catalogue which was sent seemingly to everybody by the firm of Sears Roebuck. This massive work, normally printed on reasonably flexible paper, was pierced in its top lefthand corner, threaded with string and hung in the privy on a nail:

> I'll tell you about a technical point that was put to me the other day. The question was this: 'What is the life, or how long will the average mail order catalogue last, in just the plain, ordinary eight family three holer?' It stumped me for a spell; but this bein' a reasonable question I checked up, and found that by placin' the catalogue in there, say in January – when you get your new one – you should be into the harness section by June; but, of course, that ain't through apple time, and not countin' on too many city visitors, either.
>
> An' another thing – they've been puttin' so many of those stiff-coloured sheets in the catalogue here lately that it makes it hard to figger. Somethin' really ought to done about this, and I've thought about takin' it up with Mr. Sears Roebuck hisself.

Charles Sale
THE SPECIALIST 1930

It seems that the older generation of farmer preferred using a corncob and it was the young folk who took to the catalogue but both were part of the U.S rural tradition, hence the phrase used to describe the farmlands: 'the cob and catalogue belt'

Town dwellers did their shopping in person so were not usually sent mail-order catalogues. It was their custom, until quite recent years, to collect old paper-bags, circulars, used envelopes and so on and put them away for a later session of cutting-up. This little task, as Diana Holman-Hunt remembers, was the sort of employment given to a young girl on a visit to her granny:

'Now my dear, you can make yourself useful; there are many circulars, envelopes and paper bags ready on the Moorish throne.'

'Which do you need most, spills or lavatory paper?'

'Let me see – the latter I think, as none has been made for so long. Here is your knife.' It was engraved with the name Helen Faucit. 'You will find the stiletto, the template and string in the Indian box over there.' She settled at the writing-table, and with a pin-like nib, scratched away at her letters.

I ripped the blade through the stiff paper folded round the template. 'Some of these bags from Palmer's Stores are very thick and covered with writing.'

'Print is all right on one side you know. Try not to talk.'

When I had cut a hundred sheets, I pierced their corners and threaded them with a string; I tied this in a loop to hang on a nail by the 'convenience'. I made a mental note of the softer pieces and put them together in the middle, between the back of a calendar from Barkers and an advertisement for night-lights.

Diana Holman-Hunt
MY GRANDMOTHERS AND I

When the company first put their 'toilet tissue' on the market, in the 1880s, they hit a considerable snag. Shoppers were to embarrassed to ask for it. The company overcame the problem by using an almost plain wrapper which merely gave a trade name and did not reveal what the wrapper contained. A well brought-up shopper could then, cheeks flaming, mutter 'Two, please' to the shop assistant and with a bit of luck none of her neighbours would know that she was buying a couple of rolls of That Which Must Not Be Mentioned.

Perhaps at no time was the practice of prudery brought to such a high form of art as during the reign of Queen Victoria. We all know splendid examples of this: the invention of the expression 'white meat' so that when stipulating which bit of chicken was preferred it was not necessary to say the dread word 'breast'; the titled lady who recommended that books by male and female authors should be kept on separate shelves; the hiding of lushly rounded piano legs beneath frilly drapery. The general feeling was that these were sensible precautions designed to protect the innocent and that breaking the taboos would only result in social oblivion, dizzy spells and an early death.

These taboos were at their strongest in anything to do with the natural functions performed in the bathroom (with the functions performed naturally in the bedroom a close second). In order to avoid using those words which had such earthy, beastly connotations, euphemism was piled upon euphemism. Ladies and gentlemen bent over backwards until their foreheads were (metaphorically) touching the carpet behind them to avoid mentioning, say, the china chamber pot which ladies sat upon and gentlemen stood before nightly.

Victorian delicacy of this order was the subject of a short story, rather surprisingly by an author better known for his sea-stories:

THE BEDCHAMBER MYSTERY

Now that a hundred years have passed, one of the scandals in my family can be told. It is very doubtful if in 1843 Miss Forester (she was Eulalie, but being the eldest daughter unmarried, she of course was Miss Forester) and Miss Emily Forester and Miss Eunice Forester ever foresaw the world of 1943 to which their story would be told; in fact it is inconceivable that they could have believed that there ever would be a world in which their story could be told blatantly in public print. At that time it was the sort of thing that could only be hinted at in whispers during confidential moments in feminine drawings rooms; but it was whispered about enough to reach in the end the ears of my grandfather, who was their nephew, and my grandfather told it to me.

In 1843 Miss Forester and Miss Emily and Miss Eunice Forester were already maiden ladies of a certain age. The old-fashioned Georgian house in which they lived kept itself modestly retired, just like its inhabitants, from what there was of bustle and excitement in the High Street of the market town. The ladies indeed led a retired life; they went to church a little, they visited those of the sick whom it was decent and proper for maiden ladies to visit, they read the more colourless of the novels in the circulating library, and sometimes they entertained other ladies at tea.

And once a week they entertained a man. It might almost be said that they went from week to week looking forward to those evenings. Dr. Acheson was (not one of the old ladies would have been heartless enough to say 'fortunately', but each of them felt it) a widower, and several years older even than my great-great-aunt Eulalie. Moreover, he was a keen whist player and a brilliant one, but in no way keener or more brilliant than were Eulalie, Emily, and Eunice. For years now the three nice old ladies had looked forward to their weekly evening of whist – all the ritual of setting out the green table, the two hours of silent cut-and-thrust play, and the final twenty minutes of conversation with Dr. Acheson as he drank a glass of old madeira before bidding them good night.

The late Mrs. Acheson had passed to her Maker somewhere about 1830, so that it was for thirteen years they had played their weekly game of whist before the terrible thing happened. To this day we do not know whether it happened to Eulalie or Emily or Eunice, but it happened to one of them. The three of them had retired for the night, each to her separate room, and had progressed far toward the final stage of getting into bed. They were not dried-up old spinsters; on the contrary, they were women of weight and substance, with the buxom contours even married women might have been proud of. It was her weight which was the undoing of one of them, Eulalie, Emily, or Eunice.

Through the quiet house that bedtime there sounded the crash of china and a cry of pain, and two of the sisters – which two we do not know – hurried in their dressing gowns to the bedroom of the third – her identity is uncertain – to find her bleeding profusely from severe cuts in the lower part of the back. The jagged china fragments had inflicted severe wounds, and, most unfortunately, just in those parts where the injured sister could not attend to them herself. Under the urgings of the other two she fought down her modesty sufficiently to let them attempt to deal with them, but the bleeding was profuse, and the blood of the Foresters streamed from the prone figure face downward on the bed in terrifying quantity.

'We shall have to send for the doctor,' said one of the ministering sisters; it was a shocking thing to contemplate.

'Oh, but we cannot!' said the other ministering sister.

'We must,' said the first.

'How terrible!' said the second.

And with that the injured sister twisted her neck and joined in the conversation. 'I will not have the doctor,' she said. 'I would die of shame.'

'Think of the disgrace of it!' said the second sister. 'We might even have to explain to him how it happened!'

'But she's bleeding to death,' protested the first sister.

'I'd rather die!' said the injured one, and then, as a fresh appalling thought struck her, she twisted her neck even further. 'I could never face him again. And what would happen to our whist?'

That was an aspect of the case which until then had occurred to neither of the other sisters, and it was enough to make them blench. But they were of stern stuff. Just as we do not know which was the injured one, we do not know which one thought of a way out of the difficulty, and we shall never know. We know that it was Miss Eulalie, as befitted her rank as eldest sister, who called to Deborah, the maid, to go and fetch Dr. Acheson at once, but that does not mean to say that it was not Miss Eulalie who was the injured sister – injured or not, Miss Eulalie was quite capable of calling to Deborah and telling her what to do.

As she was bid, Deborah went and fetched Dr. Acheson and conducted him to Miss Eunice's bedroom, but of course the fact that it was Miss Eunice's bedroom is really no indication that it was Miss Eunice who was in there. Dr. Acheson had no means of knowing. All he saw was a recumbent form covered by a sheet. In the center of the sheet a round hole a foot in diameter had been cut, and through the hole the seat of the injury was visible.

Dr. Acheson needed no explanations. He took his needles and his thread from his little black bag and set to work and sewed up the worst of the cuts and attended to the minor ones. Finally he straightened up and eased his aching back.

'I shall have to take those stitches out,' he explained to the still and silent figure which had borne the stitching stoically without a murmur. 'I shall come next Wednesday and do that.'

Until next Wednesday the three Misses Forester kept to their rooms. Not one of them was seen in the streets of the market town, and when on Wednesday Dr. Acheson knocked at the door Deborah conducted him once more to Miss Eunice's bedoom. There was the recumbent form, and there was the sheet with the hole in it. Dr. Acheson took out the stitches.

'It has healed very nicely,' said Dr. Acheson. 'I don't think any further attention from me will be necessary.'

The figure under the sheet said nothing, nor did Dr. Acheson expect it. He gave some concluding advice and went his way. He was glad later to receive a note penned in Miss Forester's Italian hand:

Dear Dr. Acheson,
We will all be delighted if you will come to whist this week as usual.

When Dr. Acheson arrived he found that the 'as usual' applied only to his coming, for there was a slight but subtle change in the furnishings of the drawing room. The stiff, high-backed chairs on which the three Misses Forester sat bore, each of them, a thick and comfortable cushion upon the seat. There was no knowing which of the sisters needed it.

C. S. Forester (*1899–1966*)
COSMOPOLITAN MAGAZINE, 1943

Distaste for talking about bodily functions seems to have been mainly confined to the middle-aged, and to the middle-class. Generalising wildly, it could be said that those who toil with their hands live a physical life and are not ashamed of the physics of the body, and aristocrats are above bourgeois social taboos. Similarly old folk cannot be bothered with social niceties, and children – well, children find all bodily functions fascinating and hilarious. Children have a seemingly endless repertoire of gleeful jokes, about everything that the body can get up to and should not in polite company:

> He who farts in church
> Sits in his own pew.
>
> Schoolboy joke of great age.

That particular bodily action was so natural to young children that it took years of patient persuasion to get them to stop. It seems that Nannies used a code phrase to remind the expellent that his breach of manners had been audible:

> 'Master Robert is talking German.'
>
> Quoted in NANNY SAYS.
Sir Hugh Casson and Joyce Grenfell.

'Talking German' is perhaps the one activity of those we are considering that has always been looked upon as a private rather than a social pleasure:

> Every man likes the smell of his own farts.
>
> Icelandic Proverb.
Quoted in THE FABER BOOK OF APHORISMS, 1962
ed.: W. H. Auden and Louis Kronenberger.
>
> I once accused Mr. Auden of making this up. He strongly denied it and assured me that he had come across the proverb during his tour of Iceland with Louis MacNeice in the thirties.

History records that a gentle antiquarian and writer not only enjoyed his own emanations but believed that he was giving pleasure to others:

Sir Henry Englefield had a fancy (which some greater men have had) that there was about his person a natural odour of roses and violets. Lady Grenville, hearing of this, and loving a joke, exclaimed, one day when Sir Henry was present, 'Bless me, what a smell of violets!' – 'Yes,' said he with great simplicity; 'it comes from me.'

TABLE-TALK OF SAMUEL ROGERS, 1856

The idea of achieving artificially what Sir Henry seemed to have achieved naturally had already occurred to a writer, who went on to become 'the world's most respected American'. Benjamin Franklin, infuriated by the way the Royal Academy of Brussels had belittled his discoveries, wrote a satirical letter to them (which for some reason he did not send):

A LETTER TO THE ROYAL ACADEMY OF BRUSSELS

Gentlemen:

It is universally well known that, in digesting our common food, there is created or produced in the bowels of human creatures a great quantity of wind.

That the permitting this air to escape and mix with the atmosphere is usually offensive to the company, from the fetid smell that accompanies it.

That all well-bred people, therefore, to avoid giving such offense, forcibly restrain the efforts of nature to discharge that wind.

That so retained contrary to nature it not only gives frequently great present pain, but occasions future diseases such as habitual cholics, ruptures, tympanies, etc., often destructive of the constitution, and sometimes of life itself.

Were it not for the odiously offensive smell accompanying such escapes, polite people would probably be under no more restraint in discharging such wind in company than they are in spitting or blowing their noses.

My prize question therefore should be: To discover some drug, wholesome and not disagreeable, to be mixed with our common food, or sauces, that shall render the natural discharge of wind from our bodies not only inoffensive, but agreeable as perfumes.

That this is not a chimerical project and altogether impossible, may appear from these considerations. That we already have some knowledge of means capable of *varying* that smell. He that dines on stale flesh, especially with much addition of onions, shall be able to afford a stink that no company can tolerate; while he that has lived for some time on vegetables only, shall have that breath so pure as to be insensible to the most delicate noses; and if he can manage so as to avoid the report, he may anywhere give vent to his griefs, unnoticed. But as there are many to whom an entire vegetable diet would be inconvenient, and as a little quicklime thrown into a jakes will correct the amazing quantity of fetid air arising from the vast mass of putrid matter contained in such places, and render it rather pleasing to the smell, who knows but that a little powder of lime (or some other thing equivalent), taken in our food, or perhaps a glass of limewater drunk at dinner, may have the same effect on the air produced in and issuing from our bowels? This is worth the experiment. Certain it is also that we have the power of changing by slight means the smell of another discharge, that of our water. A few stems of asparagus eaten shall give our urine a disagreeable odor; and a pill of turpentine no bigger than a pea shall bestow on it the pleasing smell of violets. And why should it be thought more impossible in nature to find means of making perfume of our wind than of our water?

For the encouragement of this inquiry (from the immortal honor to be reasonably expected by the inventor), let it be considered of how small importance to mankind, or to how small a part of mankind have been useful those discoveries in science that have heretofore made philosophers famous. Are there twenty men in Europe this day the happier, or even the easier, for any knowledge they have picked out of Aristotle? What comfort can the vortices of Descartes give to a man who has whirlwinds in his bowels! The knowledge of Newton's mutual *attraction* of the particles of matter, can it afford ease to him who is racked by their mutual *repulsion*, and the cruel distensions it occasions? The pleasure arising to a few philosophers, from seeing, a few times in their lives, the threads of light untwisted, and separated by the Newtonian prism into seven colors, can it be compared with the ease and comfort every man living might feel seven times a day, by discharging freely the wind from his bowels? Especially if it be converted into a perfume; for the pleasures of one sense being little inferior to those of another, instead of pleasing the *sight*, he might delight the *smell* of those about him, and make numbers happy, which to a benevolent mind must afford infinite satisfaction. The generous soul, who now endeavors to find out whether the friends he entertains like best claret or Burgundy, champagne or Madeira, would then inquire also whether they chose musk or

lily, rose or bergamot, and provide accordingly. And surely such a liberty of *ex-pressing one's
scentiments, and pleasing one another*, is of in-
finitely more importance to human happiness
than that liberty of the *press*, or of *abusing one
another*, which the English are so ready to fight
and die for.

In short, this invention, if completed,
would be, as Bacon expresses it, *bringing
philosophy home to men's business and bosoms.*
And I cannot but conclude that in comparison
therewith for *universal* and *continual utility*, the
science of the philosophers abovementioned,
even with the addition, gentlemen, of your
'figure quelconque,' and the figures inscribed in
it, are all together, scarcely worth a

Fart-hing

Benjamin Franklin (*1706–1790*)
Stevens Collection of Franklin Manuscripts,
State Department, Washington, D.C.

Some hundred years later, in 1882, another American wrote
on the subject, but this time a piece of fiction, an imagined
conversation at the court of Queen Elizabeth I. In 1870 Mark
Twain had married a conservative and somewhat puritanical
lady and it has been suggested that this drove underground a
natural talent for satire and revolt. At any rate in 1882 he
wrote what in those days was regarded as a 'vile' and
'unutterably coarse' story, which he managed to get printed
secretly at West Point Military Academy, to amuse his friend
the Rev. Joseph Twichell. There were originally fifty copies.
Here are the opening pages:

'1601'
Conversation, as it was by the Social Fireside in the time of the Tudors

Yesterday took Her Majesty ye Queen a fantasy such as she sometimes hath, and had to her closet certain that do write plays, books, and such like, these being my Lord Bacon, his worship Sir Walter Raleigh, Mr. Ben Jonson, and ye child Francis Beaumont, which being but sixteen, hath yet turned his hand to ye doing of ye Latin masters into our English tongue, with great discretion and much applause. Also came with these ye famous Shakespeare. A right strange mixing truly of mighty blood with mean, ye more in especial since ye Queen's Grace was present, as likewise these following, *to wit*, ye Duchess of Bilgewater, twenty-two years of age; ye Countess of Granby, twenty-six; her daughter, ye Lady Helen, fifteen; (sic) as also these two maids of honour, *to wit:* ye Lady Margery Boothy, sixty-five, and ye Lady Alice Dilberry, turned seventy, she being two years ye Queen's Grace's elder.

I being Her Majesty's cup-bearer, had no choice but to remain and behold rank forgotten, and ye high hold converse with ye low as upon equal terms, a great scandal did ye world hear thereof.

In ye heat of ye talk it befell that one did break wind, yielding an exceeding mighty and distressful stink, whereat all did laugh full sore, and then:

Ye Queen. Verily in mine eight and sixty years have I not heard ye fellow to this fart. Meseemeth, by ye great sound and clamour of it, it was male; yet ye belly it did lurk behind should now fall lean and flat against ye spine of him that hath been delivered of so stately and so vast a bulk, whereas ye guts of them that do quiff-splitters bear, stand comely still and round. Prithee, let ye author confess ye offspring. Will my Lady Alice testify?

Lady Alice. Good your Grace, an' I had room for such a thundergust within mine ancient bowls, 'tis not in reason I could discharge ye same and live to thank God for that He did choose handmaid so humble whereby to shew his power. Nay, 'tis not I that have brought forth this rich o'ermastering fog, this fragrant gloom, so pray you seek ye further.

Ye Queen. Maybe ye Lady Margery hath done ye company this favour?

Lady Margery. So please you Madam, my limbs are feeble with ye weight and drought of five and sixty winters, and it behoveth that I be tender unto them. In ye good providence of God, an' I had contained this wonder, forsooth would I have given ye whole evening of my sinking life to ye dribbling of it forth, with trembling and uneasy soul, not launched it sudden in its matchless might, taking mine own life with violence, rending my weak frame like rotten rags. It was not I, your Majesty:

Ye Queen. In God's name, who hath favoured us? Hath it come to pass that a fart shall fart *itself?* Not such a one as this, I trow. Young Master Beaumont; but no, 'twould have wafted him to Heaven like down of goose's body. 'Twas not ye little Lady Helen – nay, ne'er blush, my child; thou wilt tickle thy tender maidenhead with many a mousie-sqeak before thou learnest to blow a hurricane like to this. Wast you, my learned and ingenious Jonson?

Jonson. So fell a blast hath ne'er mine ears saluted, nor yet a stench so all-pervading and immortal. 'Twas not a novice did it, good Your Majesty, but one of veteran experience –

else had he failed of confidence. In sooth it was not I.

Ye Queen.   My Lord Bacon?

Lord Bacon.   Not from my lean entrails hath this prodigy burst forth, so please Your Grace. Naught so doth befit ye great as great performance; and haply shall ye find that 'tis not from mediocrity this miracle hath issued.

(Though ye subject be but a fart, yet will this tedious sink of learning ponderously philosophize. Meantime did ye foul and deadly stink pervade all places to that degree, that never smelt I ye like, yet dared I not to leave ye presence, albeit I was like to suffocate.)

Ye Queen.   What saith ye worshipful Master Shakespeare?

Shakespeare.   In ye great hand of God I stand, and so proclaim my innocence. Though ye sinless hosts of Heaven had foretold ye coming of this most desolating breath, proclaiming it the work of uninspired man, its quaking thunders, its firmament clogging rottenness his own achievement in due course of nature, yet had I not believed it; but had said ye pit itself hath furnished forth ye stink, and Heaven's artillery hath shook ye globe in admiration of it.

(Then was there a silence, and each did turn himself toward ye worshipful Sir Walter Raleigh, that browned embattled, bloody swashbuckler, who rising up did smile, and simpering, say:)

Sir Walter.   Most Gracious Majesty, 'twas I that did it, but indeed it was so poor and frail a note, compared with such as I am wont to furnish, that in sooth I was ashamed to call ye weakling mine in so august a presence. It was nothing – less than nothing, Madam, I did it but to clear my nether throat; but had I come prepared then had I delivered something worthy. Bear with me, please Your Grace, till I can make amends.

Mark Twain (*1835–1910*)

Mark Twain's fiction does not do justice to Queen Elizabeth. History reveals that when the same situation actually occurred the Queen managed matters with exquisite tact:

> This Earle of Oxford, making of his low obeisance
> to Queen Elizabeth, happened to let a Fart, at
> which he was so abashed and ashamed that he
> went to Travell, 7 yeares. On his return the Queen
> welcomed him home, and sayd, My Lord, I had
> forgott the Fart.

John Aubrey (1626–1697)
BRIEF LIVES. ed.: Oliver Lawson Dick

Victorians were by no means the only people to find the practice repugnant. In the early travel book *Purchas, His*

Pilgrims (II, vii, 936), 1619, there is a description of the negroes of Guinea, who were happy to wander about naked, being most upset by Netherland sailors 'who could not (or would not) hold their wind, which the natives held to be a shame and contempt done to them.'

European 'courtesy books' of the Middle Ages gave clear instructions to would-be courtiers:

> Beware of thy hinder parts from gun-blasting.
>
> BOKE OF CURTASYE, 14th. c.

But others thought differently. The Roman Emperor Claudius is reported to have considered making it socially acceptable on humanitarian grounds:

> He is reported to have had some thoughts of making a decree that it might be lawful for any man to break wind at the table, being told of a person whose modest retention had like to have cost him his life.
>
> Suetonius. (*c.A.D. 70–c. 160*)
DE VITA CAESARUM

The great medical school of the eleventh century at Salerno agreed with Claudius that retention could be a serious hazard to health:

> *To release certain winds is considered almost a*
> *   crime.*
> *Yet those who suppress them risk dropsy, convulsions,*
> *Vertigo and frightful colics.*
> *These are too often the unhappy outcome*
> *Of a sad discretion.*
>
> REGIMEN SANITATIS SALERNITATUM

Montaigne, in the sixteenth century, devoted one of his essays to contemplating his inner workings. He seems to have believed that Claudius actually did make it all legal because he wrote:

'**G**od alone knows how many times our bellies, by the refusal of one single fart, have brought us to the door of an agonising death. May the Emperor who gave us the freedom to fart where we like, also give us the power to do so.'

Michel Eyquem Montaigne (1533–1592)
ESSAIS. I.XXI.

This, perhaps ultimate, freedom was also the concern of the great French writer, Honoré de Balzac:

> 'I should like one of these days to be so well known, so popular, so celebrated, so famous, that it would permit me. . . .' Try to imagine the most enormous ambition that has entered the head of man since time began; the most impossible, the most unattainable, the most monstrous, the most Olympian, ambition; an ambition that neither Louis XIV nor Napoleon had; an ambition Alexander the Great would not have been able to satisfy in Babylon; an ambition forbidden to a dictator, to a nation's saviour, to a pope, to a master of the world. He, Balzac, said simply, '. . . so celebrated, so famous, that it would permit me to break wind in society and society would think it a most natural thing.'

JOURNAL DES GONCOURTS trans: Lewis Galantière
18 October, 1855.

Freedom was in fact spectacularly, though temporarily, achieved in France at the end of the nineteenth century. Not 'in society' or on medical grounds but on a public stage.

Oddly, a sentence in Montaigne's Essay adumbrates the whole strange phenomenon:

'That staunch upholder of will-power Saint Augustine (*Cite de Dieu* Book XIV, Chapter XXIV) claims to have seen someone in such control of his backside that he could break wind at will and follow the tone of verses spoken to him.

Michel Eyquem Montaigne (*1533–1592*)
ESSAIS, I.XXI

Modern churchmen have also held liberal views on this issue. In April 1982, the *Standard* newspaper reported that in a sermon, televised throughout the U.S.A. from the small town of Muncie, Indiana, the preacher assured his flock that 'the escape of any gas from the body is a sign that the devil is making his exit'.

In 1892 a Frenchman who billed himself as 'Le Petomane' (*péter*: to break wind) could not only follow the tone of verses with the control of his backside but perform a range of virtuoso tricks. His music-hall act was described by his son:

Before presenting the star of this story to the reader, it is important to remember the extraordinary, extravagant place which Le Petomane held in Parisian life between 1892 and 1900. 'At this time,' writes Marcel Pagnol, 'Sarah Bernhardt, Rejane, Lucien Guitry dominated the Paris stage along with the splendid Variety company the mere memory of which still makes actors who saw it when they were young feel modest and immature. These were some of the box office receipts of the time: Sarah Bernhardt 8,000 F, Lucien Guitry 6,500 F, Rejane 7,000 F, Variety 6,000 F. There was also a comic artist making himself heard at the Moulin Rouge. He seemed to be alone on the stage and his backside had more to say than his face. He called himself Le Petomane and in a single Sunday he took 20,000 F at the box office . . .'

My father was sure of himself. He had worked up his act very carefully. He would present himself in an elegant costume. Red coat with a red silk collar, breeches in black satin ruched at the knee. Black stockings and Richelieu patent leather pumps, white butterfly tie and white gloves held in the hand.

My father was never tired of telling us that he had bought this magnificent rig out of his own money and was proud of it. Contrary to what has often been said or implied, the Moulin Rouge paid not a penny towards this splendid attire, worthy of a great star.

'My children,' our father would tell us often, 'I never had stage fright before going on – not even on my opening night at the Moulin Rouge.'

The hour struck. When the compère announced 'a sensational act never before seen or heard' there was a long silence in the auditorium until the artist appeared. Then as soon as he was on, he explained what he was going to do. But, in order to get them laughing with him, he had prepared a funny little speech which I can remember word for word, having heard it so often.

This is how Le Petomane presented himself with an ease and good humour which worked beautifully on the public.

'Ladies and Gentlemen, I have the honour to present a session of Petomanie. The word Petomanie means someone who can break wind at will but don't let your nose worry you. My parents ruined themselves scenting my rectum.'

During the initial silence my father coolly began a series of small farts, naming each one 'This is a little girl, this the mother-in-law, this the bride on her wedding night (very little) and the morning after (very loud), this the mason (dry – no cement) this the dressmaker tearing two yards of calico (this one lasted at least ten seconds and imitated to perfection the sound of material being torn) then a cannon (Gunners stand by your guns! Ready – fire!) the noise of thunder, etc., etc.

Then my father would disappear for a moment behind the scenes to insert the end of a rubber tube, such as are used for enemas. It was about a yard long and he would take the other end in his fingers and in it place a cigarette which he lit. He would then smoke the cigarette as if it were in his mouth the contraction of his muscles causing the cigarette to be drawn in and then the smoke blown out. Finally my father removed the cigarette and blew out the smoke he had taken in. He then placed a little flute with six stops in the end of the tube and played one or two little tunes such as 'Le Roi Dagobert' and, of course, 'Au clair de la lune'. To end the act he removed the flute and then blew out several gas jets in the footlights with some force. Then he invited the audience to sing in chorus with him.

From the beginning of the 'audition' mad laughter had come. This soon built up into general applause. The public and especially women fell about laughing. They would cry from laughing. Many fainted and fell down and had to be resuscitated.

'This was all splendid for me,' my father said, 'the whole of my act went across without a hitch and full steam ahead.'

The director enthusiastically offered my father a month's contract renewable. And since his triumph grew all the time, neither side delayed signing a contract which bound them for several years with the right for Le Petomane to play abroad or elsewhere in France.

My father installed his family in a turreted chalet in Saint Maur des Fosses. There we had servants, who became at the same time friends, and in particular a coachman-cum-valet, Pitalugue, who also acted as my father's manager.

He had a pretty little English carriage, a cabriolet drawn by a mare called Aida and when he drove it himself all dressed up in his best, with Le Petomane in the driver's seat, he was recognised and saluted affectionately as an important personage wherever he went:

'That's Le Petomane who went past then . . . !'

He was the talk of the town.

Jean Nohain and F. Caradec
LE PETOMANE. 1967. trans.: Warren Tute.

Proceeding on our tour of the bathroom, we have examined the bath and ruminated on the washbasin and its Assorted Toiletries. We should now be faced with the bidet but in Britain this is highly unlikely. For some reason the Island Race has never been able to take seriously this useful and efficient adjunct to personal hygiene. Instead, when met with on continental holidays it gives rise either to a shudder of distaste at the strange practices which foreigners get up to or thigh-slapping jokes about 'the doll's bath' and 'so that's where we're supposed to wash our feet'.

Suffice it to say that the first mention of a bidet was made in 1710, in France of course, when it was reported that Marc René de Voyer, Marquis d'Argenson, lieutenant of the Paris police, was graciously received by Madame de Prie whilst she was astride her bidet. Though how he knew what she was astride considering the voluminous skirts of the period raises doubts. She might just as well have been astride a unicycle.

So leaping lightly over the bidet, or where it would have been had there been one, we arrive at what the French sometimes call *le petit coin*. There in the corner It stands. The porcelain bowl with its seat and lid.

The lavatory/loo/bog/john/can/dunny/W.C./*le double*/toilet/comfort-station/doings/gents/penny-house/carsey.

The modern domestic Thing is, as it were, dual purpose

and normally is happy to accept the products of both the minor and the major natural functions.

I say 'normally' because local customs can vary. The actress Gretchen Franklyn recalls arriving at a Theatrical boarding-house in the North-East of England which boasted a 'toilet' downstairs and another on the top landing. Anxious to make herself comfortable after her journey she tactfully made for the one at the top of the stairs. As she mounted the stairs there came a pounding on the banisters and the voice of the landlady rose up the stairwell 'We doan't use that toilet for solids, dear'.

Performance of the minor – or non-solids – natural function crops up frequently in tribal myth and legend. It is recorded that the Ancient Celts elected Maeve as their queen because she won a contest to see which of the tribal maidens could squat down and make the biggest hole in the snow. They later murdered her but perhaps for another reason.

The contest was echoed in modern times during the last war. Professor R. V. Jones, the scientist who 'bent the beam', reveals in his book *Most Secret War* that he won a male version of the Celts' competition by peeing over a six-foot wall.

Tribes living in warm climates formulated sensible rules of personal hygiene. In the old Testament, in Deuteronomy, it is recommended that a spot be chosen well away from the tents, a hole be dug with a mattock and filled in again afterwards – a routine still practised by army patrols and cats.

A Greek didactic poet penned some helpful hints for gentlemen:

When you would have your urine pass away,
Stand not upright before the eye of day;
And scatter not your water as you go
Nor let it, when you're naked, from you flow:
In either case 'tis an unseemly sight:
The gods observe alike by day and night:
The man whom we devout and wise may call
Sits in that act, or streams against a wall.

Hesiod (*c. 8th century B.C.*)
WORKS AND DAYS. trans.: Thomas Cooke

Pliny, in *Naturalis Historia*, quoted Ostanes as saying that to allow a little urine to fall upon the foot in the morning was beneficial to health. So according to Hesiod and Ostanes the old Corsican I once saw turning away from the wall of a church buttoning his flies, his left boot damp and shiny, was both devout and healthy. But not law-abiding. Above his head on the wall of the church a large notice said *Défense d'uriner contre le mur de l'église.*

Instructions as to where to dig and where to stand are all very well but they presuppose that there is plenty of time in hand and everything is under control, which is not always so:

Adrian Mitchell's Famous Weak Bladder Blues

Now some praise God because he gave us the
    bomb to drop in 1945
But I thank the Lord for equipping me with the
    fastest cock alive.

You may think a sten-gun's frequent, you can call
    greased lightning fast,
But race them down to the Piccadilly bog and
    watch me zooming past.

Well it's excuse me,
And I'll be back.
Door locked so rat-a-tat-tat.
You mind if I go first?
I'm holding this cloudburst.
I'll be out in 3·7 seconds flat.

I've got the Adamant Trophy, the Niagara Cup,
    you should see me on the M.1 run,
For at every comfort station I've got a reputation .
    for – doing the ton.

Once I met that Speedy Gonzales and he was first
    through the door.
But I was unzipped, let rip, zipped again and out
    before he could even draw.

Now God killed Vicky and he let Harold Wilson
    survive,
But the good Lord blessed little Adrian Mitchell
    with the fastest cock alive.

Adrian Mitchell
OUT LOUD, 1968

Others who are not able to choose either the time or place
are young children Going Through a Phase:

A dry bed deserves a boiled sweet.

NANNY SAYS, Hugh Casson and Joyce Grenfell

Sleeping next to a child who is soaking wet and steaming
seems an odd thing to be nostalgic about but an American
poet and journalist managed it:

When Willie was a little boy,
    Not more than five or six,
Right constantly he did annoy
    His mother with his tricks.
Yet not a picayune cared I
    For what he did or said
Unless, as happened frequently,
    The rascal wet the bed.

Closely he cuddled up to me
    And put his hand in mine,
Till all at once I seemed to be
    Afloat in seas of brine.
Sabean odors clogged the air
    And filled my soul with dread,
Yet I could only grin and bear
    When Willie wet the bed.

'Tis many times that rascal has
    Soaked all the bedclothes through,
Whereat I'd feebly light the gas
    And wonder what to do.

Yet there he lay, so peaceful-like,
 God bless his curly head!
I quite forgave the little tyke
 For wetting of the bed.

Ah, me! those happy days have flown,
 My boy's a father too,
And little Willies of his own
 Do what he used to do.
And I, ah! all that's left for me
 Are dreams of pleasure fled;
My life's not what it used to be
 When Willie wet the bed!

Eugene Field (1850–1895)

> It was Eugene Field, reviewing a production of *King Lear*, who
> wrote of Creston Clarke: 'He played the King as though under
> momentary apprehension that someone else was about to play
> the ace.'

The indiscriminate showering of the natural blessings was
not confined to Corsicans, incontinent poets and small
children but popped up throughout history, in fact and in
fiction.

There was the giant Gargantua, whose mighty effusion
resulted in a noble city being renamed:

> Some few days after that they had refreshed
> themselves, he went to see the city, and was
> beheld of everybody there with great admiration:
> for the people of Paris are such fools, such
> puppies, and naturals, that a juggler, a carrier of
> indulgencies, a sumpter-horse, a mule with his
> bells, a blind fiddler in the middle of a cross lane,
> shall draw a greater confluence of people together
> than an evangelical preacher. And they pressed so
> hard upon him, that he was constrained to rest
> himself upon the steeple of our Lady's church; at
> which place, seeing so many about him, he said
> with a loud voice, 'I believe that these buzzards

will have me to pay them here my welcome hither, and my beverage: it is but good reason. I will now give them their wine, but it shall be only a *par ris*, that is, in sport.' Then smiling, he untied his goodly codpiece, and lugging out his Roger into the open air, he so bitterly all-to-be-pissed them, that he drowned two hundred and sixty thousand four hundred and eighteen, besides the women and little children.

Some, nevertheless, of the company escaped this piss-flood by mere speed of foot, who when they were at the higher end of the university, sweating, coughing, spitting, and out of breath, they began to swear and curse, some in good hot earnest, and others *par ris*, *carimari*, *carimara*; *golynoly*, *golynolo*; 'ods-bodkins, we are washed *par ris*,' from whence the city hath been ever since called Paris.

François Rabelais (*1495?–1553*)
THE BOOK OF GARGANTUA. trans.: Sir Thomas Urquhart
and Peter Motteux

Perhaps it was this story which put an Italian gentleman off:

The pleasantest dotage that ever I read, saith *Laurentius*, was of a Gentleman at *Senes* in *Italy* who was afraid to pisse, lest all the towne should bee drowned; the Physicians caused the bells to be rung backward, and told him the towne was on fire, whereupon he made water, and was immediately cured.

Robert Burton (*1577–1640*)
ANATOMY OF MELANCHOLY

And perhaps reading Burton gave Dean Swift an idea for a way in which Lemuel Gulliver could render the King of Lilliput a most signal service:

I was alarmed at Midnight with the Cries of many Hundred People at my Door; by which

112

being suddenly awaked, I was in some Kind of Terror. I heard the Word *Burglum* repeated incessantly; several of the Emperor's Court making their Way through the Croud, intreated me to come immediately to the Palace, where her Imperial Majesty's Apartment was on fire, by the Carelessness of a Maid of Honour, who fell asleep while she was reading a Romance. I got up in an Instant; and Orders being given to clear the Way before me; and it being likewise a Moonshine Night, I made a shift to get to the Palace without trampling on any of the People. I found they had already applied Ladders to the Walls of the Apartment, and were well provided with Buckets, but the Water was at some Distance. These Buckets were about the Size of a large Thimble, and the poor People supplied me with them as fast as they could; but the Flame was so violent, that they did little Good. I might easily have stifled it with my Coat, which I unfortunately left behind me for haste, and came away only in my Leather Jerkin. The Case seemed wholly desperate and deplorable; and this magnificent Palace would have infallibly been burnt down to the Ground, if, by a Presence of Mind, unusual to me, I had not suddenly thought of an Expedient. I had the Evening before drank plentifully of a most delicious Wine, called *Glimigrim*, (the *Blefuscudians* called it *Flunec*, but ours is esteemed the better Sort) which is very diuretick. By the luckiest Chance in the World, I had not discharged myself of any Part of it. The Heat I had contracted by coming very near the Flames, and by my labouring to quench them, made the Wine begin to operate by Urine; which I voided in such a Quantity, and applied so well to the proper Places, that in three Minutes the Fire was wholly extinguished; and the

rest of that noble Pile, which had cost so many
Ages in erecting, preserved from Destruction.

Jonathan Swift (*1667–1745*)
GULLIVER'S TRAVELS

These passages would hardly have surprised or shocked
most eighteenth-century readers. Ladies were accustomed to
relieving themselves discreetly almost anywhere. Until the
early nineteenth century they wore long dresses and no
drawers so it was simply a matter of standing astride some sort
of gutter and gazing dreamily about for a minute or so. In
extremely cold climates where gutters were frozen more
sophisticated measures were called for. Marco Polo writes that
in Siberia it became fashionable for a lady's serving-maid to
follow her mistress carrying a large sponge which she could,
without indelicacy, insert beneath her lady's dress to absorb
the effluent.

Gentlemen did the best they could in the circumstances.
For instance, during troop manoeuvres:

> M. de Vendôme (I report only the bare,
> unvarnished facts) arrived independently at Ghent
> between seven and eight o'clock in the morning,
> as troops were entering the town. He stopped with
> the remnant of his suite still accompanying him,
> dismounted, let down his breeches, and there and
> then planted his stools quite close to the troops as
> he watched them go by.

Duc de Saint-Simon (*1675–1755*)
HISTORICAL MEMOIRS, trans. Lucy Norton

After a jolly party:

> Sir Charles Sedley, Bart., sometimes of Wadham
> coll., Charles lord Buckhurst (afterwards earl of
> Middlesex), Sir Thom Ogle, &c. were at a cook's
> house, at the signe of the cock in Bow-street neare
> Covent-garden, within the libertie of Westminster;

and being all inflamed with strong liquors, they
went into the balcony, joyning to their chamber-
window, and putting downe their breeches, they
excrementized in the street.

Anthony Wood (*1632–1695*)
LIFE AND TIMES

A noted Puritan divine in skittish mood became quite
inventive:

Of Dr. Thomas Goodwin, when ffelow of
Catherine Hall. – He was somewhat whimsycall, in
a frolic pist once in old Mr. Lothian's pocket.

Thomas Woodcock (*fl. 1695*)
PAPERS

While an aristocratic lady at the Court of Louis XIV at
Versailles must have been less than a social asset at dinner
parties:

The Princesse d'Harcourt ... was a
glutton, and so eager to relieve herself
that she drove her hostesses to desper-
ation, for although she never denied herself
the use of the convenience on leaving table,
she sometimes allowed herself no time to
reach it at leisure, leaving a dreadful trail
behind her that made the servants of M. du
Maine and M. le Grand wish her to the devil.
As for her, she was never in the least embarrassed, but lifted her skirts and went her way,
saying on her return that she had felt a little
faint.

Duc de Saint-Simon (*1675–1755*)
HISTORICAL MEMOIRS, trans.: Lucy Norton

115

Mademoiselle de Montpensier, and the Palatine Duchess of Orléans, though women of the highest birth and rank, as well as of unimpeached conduct, conceal nothing on these points, in their writings. The former, speaking of the Duchess of Orléans, her step-mother, second wife of Gaston, brother of Louis the Thirteenth, says, 'She had contracted a singular habit of always running into another room, *pour se placer sur la Chaise percée*, when dinner was announced. As she never failed in this particular, the Grand Maître, or Lord Steward of Gaston's Household, who performed the ceremony of summoning their Royal Highnesses to table; observed, smelling to his Baton of office, that there must certainly be either Senna or Rhubarb in its composition, as it invariably produced the effect of sending the Duchess to the Garderobe.' I have, myself, seen the late Electress Dowager of Saxony, daughter of the Emperor Charles the Seventh, at her own palace, in the suburbs of Dresden, rise from the table where she was playing, when the room has been full of company of both sexes; lay down her cards, retire for a few minutes, during which time the game was suspended, and then return, observing to those near her, '*J'ai pris Médecine aujourd'huy.*'

Sir Nathaniel Wraxall (1751–1831)
HISTORICAL MEMOIRS

Other memoirs and diaries give similar accounts of courtiers using the walls of the Hall of Mirrors, corners of staircases, in fact any part of the building where they were unobserved by the King. The custom at Fontainebleau was to wait until dusk and then make for a lawn outside. Here lords, ladies and the Swiss Guard would assemble, each trying to ignore the other and get on with his or her business. The pretty walks became unwalkable.

The English Court was almost as bad in its habits. When the plague slackened its grip and the Court of King Charles II gave up living in Oxford and returned to London, a university diarist recorded:

> To give a further character of the court, they,
> though they were neat and gay in their apparell,
> yet they were very nasty and beastly, leaving at
> their departure their excrements in every corner,
> in chimneys, studies, colehouses, cellers.

Anthony Wood (1632–1695)
LIFE AND TIMES

Not all recorded examples of this sort of thing show gross slovenliness of manners or drunken caperings. There was the episode concerning a Lady and the minister of Thames Ditton, the Rev. George Harvest. Mr. Harvest was in every way well-mannered and gentlemanly. But he was extremely absent minded:

> One day Lady Onslow, being desirous of knowing
> the most remarkable planets and constellations,

requested Mr. Harvest, on a fine starlight night, to
point them out to her, which he undertook to do;
but in the midst of his lecture, having occasion to
make water, thought that need not interrupt it,
and accordingly directing that operation with one
hand, went on in his explanation, pointing out the
constellations with the other.

Francis Grose (*1731–1791*)
THE OLIO

It was not that our male ancestors had no place to Go.
There had always been areas and rooms allocated for their
relief; the Palace of Versailles had many, as had the colleges of
Oxford. The problem was to get gentlemen to use them.
Gentlemen, endowed by nature with directional control, had
developed over the centuries a tradition of using whatever was
at hand rather than what was especially provided for the
purpose. In the early years of the last century Lord Byron was
banned from Long's Hotel in Bond Street for peeing in a
corner of the entrance hall rather than going to the bother of
seeking out a necessary house.

It is recorded that at a meeting of clergy in the 1920s at an
Oxford college a rather hearty young vicar asked whether it
was permitted to pee in the bedroom basin. 'Certainly not!'
said the Dean. Adding, after thought, 'Unless the window is
closed.'

It seems that this male privilege is tolerated, under certain
conditions, in the clubland of St. James's where one gentle-
man's club has a notice, I am told, reading DURING THE
ASPARAGUS SEASON MEMBERS ARE REQUESTED
NOT TO RELIEVE THEMSELVES IN THE HAT-
STAND.

It was a simple matter for people who lived in the country
to allocate a special place; they had plenty of room. Like the
biblical hole in the ground which was well away from the
tents, the hole they dug was well away, and down wind, from
their dwelling. The next development was to put a hut round
the hole, partly to stop the pig falling in but also for protection
against the weather. It came to be called the 'privy' (or in

Tudor times, the 'jakes', probably from 'Jack's place', Jack being the nickname for a simple countryman). The countryman's privy was not only a convenient and fairly hygienic answer to the problem but was also a considerable asset to his kitchen garden:

> The privy had from time immemorial been an important source of soil fertility. By the mid-nineteenth century human urine and excrement had been subjected to scientific analysis. *The Cottage Gardener* published the fascinating fact that 'the annual urine of two men is said to contain sufficient mineral food for an acre of land, and mixed with ashes will produce a fair crop of turnips'. When the shed at the bottom of the garden was supplanted by indoor plumbing the cottage garden was the poorer. I myself often stayed as a child in a cottage with an outdoor privy where squares cut from the *Daily Mail* and a bucket of ashes were placed beside the seat. All was used on the garden which grew, I remember, spectacularly good runner beans.
>
> Anne Scott-James (*1913–*   )
> THE COTTAGE GARDEN

It was usual for the cottager to shift his privy from time to time so that the whole of his garden enjoyed the benefit. When the structure had to be permanent the resultant soil could become very rich indeed:

> In [New] Colledge, the house of office or Bog-house is a famous pile of building, the dung of it computed by old Jacob Bobart to be worth a great deal of money, who said this Compost when rotton was an excellent soil to fill deep holes to plant young vines.
>
> Thomas Baskerville (*c. 1675*)

119

A drawback to the privy was that not only the domestic pig was in danger of falling in. The principle was that the occupier was suspended above the hole in the ground on a wooden pole, or plank, or a seat with a hole cut in it. And wood rots. Or is not strong enough to support the weight suddenly applied to it:

> 'And when it comes to construction,' I sez, 'I can
> give you joists or beams. Joists make a good job.
> Beams cost a bit more, but they're worth it.
> Beams, you might say, will last forever. 'Course, I
> could give you joists, but take your Aunt Emmy,
> she ain't gettin' a mite lighter. Some day she might
> be out there when them joists give away and there
> she'd be – catched. Another thing you've got to
> figger on, Elmer,' I sez, 'is that Odd Fellows picnic
> in the fall. Them boys is goin' to get in there in
> fours and sixes, singin' and drinkin', and the like,
> and I want to tell you there's nothin' breaks up an
> Odd Fellows picnic quicker than a diggin' party.'

Charles Sale
THE SPECIALIST

Records show that diggin' parties were required fairly frequently. A famous royal catastrophe occurred in 1184 when the Emperor Frederick I summoned a group of notables, including eight ruling princes, to a Diet in the Great Hall at Erfurt:

> The Emperor . . . had occasion to go to the
> privy, whither he was followed by some of the
> nobles, when suddenly the floor that was under
> them began to sink; the emperor immediately took
> hold of the iron grates of a window, whereat he
> hung by the hands till some came and succoured
> him. Some gentlemen fell to the bottom where
> they perished. And it is most observable, that
> amongst those who died was Henry earl of

Schwartzenburg, who carried the presage of his
death in a common imprecation of his, which was
this, *If I do it not, I wish I may sink in a privy.*

Rev. Nathaniel Wanley *(1634–1680)*
THE WONDERS OF THE LITTLE WORLD

One sad incident concerned a gentleman who fell in on an
inappropriate day:

> A Jewe at Tewkesbury fell into a Privie on the
> Saturday and would not that day bee taken out for
> reverence of his sabbath, wherefore Richard Clare
> Earle of Glocester kepte him there till Munday
> that he was dead.

John Stowe *(1525?–1605)*
A SURVEY OF LONDON, 1603.

Reverence for the sabbath was still strong in the 1890s but
the threat to life and limb was much smaller and awkward
dilemmas could be dealt with tactfully:

> A lady got locked into the lavatory on a Sunday
> morning; so her brother-in-law, a clergyman, sat on
> a chair up against the door and read the morning
> service aloud to her from outside.

Gwen Raverat *(1885–1957)*
PERIOD PIECE: A CAMBRIDGE CHILDHOOD

It is encouraging to learn that a nasty experience in a House
of Office resulted in at least one spiritual awakening:

WILLIAM TWISSE

His sonne Dr. Twisse, Minister of the New-
church neer Tothill-street Westminster, told me,
that he had heard his father say, that when he was
a schoole-boy at Winton-college, that he was a
rakell; and that one of his Schoolefellowes and
camerades (as wild as himselfe) dyed there; and

that, his father goeing in the night to the House of
office, the phantome or Ghost of his dead
schoolefellow appeared to him, and told him *I am
damn'd*: and that this was the Beginning of his
Conversion.

John Aubrey (*1626–1697*)
BRIEF LIVES, ed. Oliver Lawson Dick

The misfortune of falling into the privy – or perhaps the
fear of it happening – was so prevalent that it gave rise to a
popular limerick:

> There was a young man from Kilbride
> Who fell in a privy and died.
> His broken-hearted brother
> Fell into another,
> And now they're interred side by side.

Anon.
Quoted in THE LIMERICK, ed. G. Legman

The backyard privy has by no means disappeared, particularly in rural areas, but it is no longer such a cornerstone of
family life as it once was. Poets, especially American poets,
sigh for the memory of those dear, dead days with –
considering sentiments like 'I ween the old familiar smell will
sooth my jaded soul' – what might be called *nostalgie de la ph-
e-e-e-w:*

> When memory keeps me company and moves to
>   smiles or tears,
> A weather-beaten object looms through the mist of
>   years.
> Behind the house and barn it stood, a hundred
>   yards or more,
> And hurrying feet a path had made, straight to its
>   swinging door.
> Its architecture was a type of simple classic art,
> But in the tragedy of life it played a leading part.

And oft the passing traveller drove slow, and
    heaved a sigh,
To see the modest hired girl slip out with glances
    shy.

We had our posey garden that the women loved so
    well,
I loved it, too, but better still I loved the stronger
    smell
That filled the evening breezes so full of homely
    cheer,
And told the night-o'ertaken tramp that human life
    was near.
On lazy August afternoons, it made a little bower
Delightful, where my grandsire sat and whiled
    away an hour.
For there the morning-glory its very eaves
    entwined,
And berry bushes reddened in the steaming soil
    behind.

All day fat spiders spun their webs to catch the
    buzzing flies
That flitted to and from the house, where Ma was
    baking pies.
And once a swarm of hornets bold, had built a
    palace there,
And stung my unsuspecting aunt – I must not tell
    you where.
Then Father took a flaming pole – that was a
    happy day –
He nearly burned the building up, but the hornets
    left to stay.
When summer bloom began to fade and winter to
    carouse
We banked the little building with a heap of
    hemlock boughs.

But when the crust was on the snow and the sullen
    skies were gray,
In sooth the building was no place where one could
    wish to stay.
We did our duties promptly, there one purpose
    swayed the mind;
We tarried not, nor lingered long on what we left
    behind.
The torture of that icy seat would make a Spartan
    sob,
For needs must scrape the goose flesh with a
    lacerating cob,
That from a frost-encrusted nail, was suspended
    by a string –
For Father was a frugal man and wasted not a
    thing.

When Grandpa had to 'go out back' and make his
    morning call,
We'd bundle up the dear old man with a muffler
    and a shawl,
I knew the hole on which he sat – 'twas padded all
    around,
And once I dared to sit there – 'twas all too wide I
    found.
My loins were all too little, and I jackknifed there
    to stay,
They had to come and get me out, or I'd have
    passed away.
Then Father said ambition was a thing that boys
    should shun,
And I just used the children's hole 'till childhood
    days were done.

And still I marvel at the craft that cut those holes so
    true,
The baby hole, and the slender hole that fitted
    Sister Sue;

124

That dear old country landmark! I've tramped
    around a bit,
And in the lap of luxury my lot has been to sit,
But ere I die I'll eat the fruit of trees I robbed of
    yore,
Then seek the shanty where my name is carved
    upon the door.
I ween the old familiar smell will sooth my jaded
    soul,
I'm now a man, but none the less, I'll try the
    children's hole.

James Whitcomb Riley (*1849–1916*)
THE OLD BACKHOUSE

Vastly more complicated sewage-disposal problems arose for town dwellers. The rich and the mighty had little trouble, of course, with an army of servants and plenty of space. Monasteries, invariably sited near running water, sat their monks in rows above a conduit. Castles had privies built into the thickness of the walls, with a channel to lead the effluent down the outside of the wall and into the moat. But as the water in moats was usually static this could produce problems. Owners of yachts still have the same problem today when they are tied up alongside each other in harbour or in a marina, all pumping their sewage overboard. Noël Coward defined the problem when he reappeared on the deck of a friend's boat after a visit to the ship's 'toilet' and said 'Not so much "good-bye" as "au revoir"'.

Many owners of great mansions had huge drains dug which led the waste well away from the house and into a stream (some of these were discovered later and were claimed to be secret passages). Other noble houses had little rooms specially built behind fire-places for warmth or tucked away where they would avoid embarrassment (to be claimed later as priest-holes and secret rooms). Almost all of them were unventilated and must have been appalling to use.

Even today, in the hot climate of a Greek island a privy represents a considerable health hazard:

Nimiec . . . arrived at a fishing village in Merlera on one of his fishing jaunts, and was housed in a small cottage with an earth lavatory, primitive and so full of flies that he drew the attention of his host to its condition. His host said briskly, 'Flies? Of course there are flies. If you could do as we all do and wait until just before the midday meal you would not find a fly in the lavatory. They all come round to the kitchen.'

Lawrence Durrell
PROSPERO'S CELL

Monarchs and the Gentry got round the problem of having to sit in a reeking privy by having the privy brought to their chamber in portable form and then having it smartly taken away again after use. These portable privies were called 'close stools' (In France, *'chaise percée'*, i.e. chair with a hole in it), and royal close stools were sumptuously decorated. Samuel Johnson did not approve of an elegant stool which Boswell had seen at an Embassy in Paris:

'Sir, that is Dutch; quilted seats retain a bad smell. No Sir, there is nothing so good as the plain board.'

BOSWELL'S JOURNAL OF A TOUR TO THE HEBRIDES WITH SAMUEL JOHNSON, ed. F. A. Pottle and C. H. Bennett

A simpler, even more portable, version of the close stool was the chamber-pot, which could be kept handy in the dining-room or salon and used almost anywhere, frequently behind a screen so that conversation need not be interrupted.

The British used them widely. Judges often kept a porcelain pot below their bench. Travellers took their own pot for use during long journeys by coach.

A noble gentleman once sent a china chamber-pot as a gift to the Countess of Hillsborough. Attached was a short explanatory poem:

Too proud, too delicate to tell her wants
Her lover guesses them, and gladly grants;

The wish that he still trembles to explain
She long has known but bids him wish in vain;
With tears incessant he laments his case,
And can have small occasion for this vase.
Go then beneath her bed or toilet stand,
But chiefly after tea be near at hand;
Sure of her notice then, then take your fill,
Nor fear one drop her tidy hand should spill,
Though Cyder or Champagne supply the source,
And laughter hurry forth the rapid course.
Who talks of the Pierian spring or stream?
But stop dear Muse, lest on th'enchanting theme
My warm imagination should proceed
To what you must not write, she must not read.

Henry Fox, Lord Holland (*1705–1774*)
Kings-gate, 1764

The chamber-pot no longer exists but Lord Holland's house at
Kingsgate, Kent, or what is left of the house, still stands. It lies
back from the road opposite Joss Bay.

The use of some sort of small portable receptacle goes back
many centuries. The Unspeakable Trimalchio in ancient
Rome used one at the public baths:

Suddenly we saw a bald old man in a reddish
shirt, playing ball with some long-haired boys. It
was not so much the boys that made us watch,
although they alone were worth the trouble, but
the old gentleman himself. He was taking his
exercise in slippers and throwing a green ball
around. But he didn't pick it up if it touched the
ground; instead there was a slave holding a bagful,
and he supplied them to the players. We noticed
other novelties. Two eunuchs stood around at
different points: one of them carried a silver
chamber pot, the other counted the balls, not
those flying from hand to hand according to the
rules, but those that fell to the ground. We were
still admiring these elegant arrangements when

Menelaus hurried up to us.

'This is the man you'll be dining with,' he said. 'In fact; you are now watching the beginning of the dinner.'

No sooner had Menelaus spoken than Trimalchio snapped his fingers. At the signal the eunuch brought up the chamber pot for him, while he went on playing. With the weight off his bladder, he demanded water for his hands, splashed a few drops on his fingers and wiped them on a boy's head.

Petronius (*fl. 1st century A.D.*)
THE SATYRICON, trans.: John Sullivan

Inhabitants of hot climes had little interest in chamber-pots but those who dwelt midst ice and snow and could not nip out in the night to a convenient patch of *maquis* or rain-forest knew their worth. As a writer found when he bedded down with some Eskimos in their igloo:

I slipped into my fur bag. The children squeezed themselves under the skins, and the wrinkled granny, grumbling and complaining like any old lady, squatted on her heels and stripped off all her clothes. She got into bed, muttering to herself and grunting, tossing about for a while before she fell asleep. Ayallik, meanwhile, had stripped to the nude. With a cheerful 'Alapa!' . . . 'Cold!' he vanished under his covers. Ongirlak was the last to go to bed. She plugged the door-hole with a snow block and fixed her lamps for the night, beating out all of the flame except for a tiny glow in the corner, a night-light. Then she distributed small empty tins, improvised chamber-pots, placing one at each of our heads.

Roger P. Buliard
INUK

The French had always used chamber-pots and had even invented a special female version. At the time of Louis XIV there was a Jesuit preacher at Versailles whose sermons were of such an inordinate length that ladies could not last the course, so someone invented a china container, shaped like a large sauce-boat without a lip, which they could secrete beneath their skirts (dexterity must have been needed when leaving the church). The famous Jesuit preacher was Louis Bourdaloue and it seems only proper that the pot, which brought comfort and ease to many of the ladies of his congregation, should have been named a *bourdaloue*. Examples can still be found in junk shops, cottage hospitals and homes, usually filled with flowers or gravy.

It seems that coping with nature's needs was not all that difficult for countrymen, Kings, Eskimos, and anybody who was rich. Privacy was not a major problem because very few sought it. Communal privies, family privies and two and three seaters were normal and the 'house of necessity', or whatever it was called at the time, was a convivial place where husband and wife went together and strangers exchanged gossip; you were not expected to be in there alone:

> *You may, as your great French lord doth, invite some special friend of yours from the table, to hold discourse with you as you sit in that with-drawing-chamber.*
>
> Thomas Dekker (*c. 1570–c. 1641*)
> GULL'S HORNBOOK

The French were noted for their gregariousness whilst on stool. The novelist Smollett was most alarmed at the practice and its implications:

I have known a lady handed to the house of office by her admirer, who stood at the door, and entertained her with *bons mots* all the time she was within. But I should be glad to know, whether it is possible for a fine lady to speak and act in this manner, without exciting ideas to her own disadvantage in the mind of every man who has any imagination left, and enjoys the intire use of his senses, howsoever she may be authorised by the customs of her country?

Tobias Smollett (*1721–1771*)
TRAVELS THROUGH FRANCE AND ITALY

Although our Kings and Princes received guests while they were at stool, the practice was particularly widespread at the French court:

> The Duc d'Humières asked if I would take him
> one morning to Versailles, as he wished to thank
> M. le Duc D'Orléans. The Regent was not dressed
> when we arrived, but still in the cupboard under
> the stairs, which he had made his privy. I found
> him there, sitting on his *chaise percée*, surrounded
> by two or three of his gentlemen and valets.

Duc de Saint-Simon (*1675–1755*)
HISTORICAL MEMOIRS, trans. Lucy Norton

Being in company with a Great Man in such intimate circumstances was most useful in the elaborate game of gaining preferment at Versailles:

> The Abbé Jules, later Cardinal, Alberoni wormed
> himself into Vendôme's confidence by making
> delicious cheese soup and pandering to his
> revolting habits. Saint-Simon says that he once
> exclaimed, 'Oh! Angelic bottom!', when Vendôme
> rose from his *chaise-percée*.

Duc de Saint-Simon (*1675–1755*)
HISTORICAL MEMOIRS, trans. Lucy Norton
Note by Lucy Norton, Chap. XVIII

Gregariousness at stool was also the custom in Italy, as a young English traveller noted when staying in Naples with Sir William and Lady Hamilton. Acts and functions which were studiously concealed in England he found openly performed at the court of Ferdinand IV of Naples:

> When the King has made a hearty meal, and feels an inclination to retire, he commonly communicates that intention to the Noblemen around him in waiting, and selects the favoured individuals, whom, as a mark of predilection, he chooses shall attend him. '*Sono ben pransato*,' says he, laying his hand on his belly, '*Adesso bisogna un buona panchiata.*' The persons thus preferred, then accompany his Majesty, stand respectfully round him, and amuse him by their conversation, during the performance.

Sir Nathaniel Wraxall (*1751–1831*)
HISTORICAL MEMOIRS

The young Sir Nathaniel, fired by these discoveries of continental practices hitherto unmentionable in polite society, went on to make a little list of sordid behaviour in French royalist circles:

> Henry the Third, it is well known, was stabbed in the belly, of which wound he died, in 1589, while sitting on the *Chaise percée*; in which indecorous situation he did not scruple to give audience to Clement, the regicide Monk, who assassinated him. Marshal Suarrow, in our own time, received his Aides du Camp and his General Officers, precisely in a similar manner. Madame de Maintenon, as the Duke de St. Simon informs us, thought those moments so precious, that she commonly accompanied Louis the Fourteenth to the 'Garderobe'. So did Louvois, when Minister of State. The Duke de Vendôme, while commanding the

Armies of France in Spain and Italy, at the commencement of the last Century, was accustomed to receive the greatest personages, on public business, in the same situation. We have Cardinal Alberoni's authority for this fact. If we read the account written by Du Bois, of the last illness of Louis the Thirteenth, we may there see what humiliating functions Anne of Austria performed for that Prince in the course of his malady; over which an English writer, more fastidious, would have drawn a veil.

Ibid.

The real sufferers from the problem of where to Go were poor people who increasingly began to congregate in towns. Here there were no fields or bushes to disappear into, no running water to dispose of the end product. Everybody had a fairly noisome time of it in towns but at least the wealthier had their close-stools and their privies (into which the close-stools and the chamber-pots were emptied) but, as in Pepys' house, these were usually in the basement or under the stairs and had to be dug out and carried through the house at night by 'dung-farmers'.

The poor, living in rookeries of lodgings, usually had no facilities at all within the house. There were public 'necessary houses' but the nearest might be a mile away. It was customary to use chamber-pots and just empty them into the roadway.

In Edinburgh, where there were no public and very few private privies, most of the population lived in tall tenement buildings and a special tradition of pot-emptying evolved:

On six evenings of the week the taverns were filled with men of all classes at their ale and claret, till the ten o'clock drum, beaten at the order of the magistrates, warned every man that he must be off home. Then were the High Street and Canongate filled with parties of every description, hurrying

132

unsteadily along, High Court Judges striving to walk straight as became their dignity, rough Highland porters swearing in Gaelic as they forced a passage for their sedan-chairs, while far overhead the windows opened, five, six, or ten storeys in the air, and the close stools of Edinburgh discharged the collected filth of the last twenty-four hours into the street. It was good manners for those above to cry 'Gardy-loo' (*gardez l'eau*) before throwing. The returning roysterer cried back 'Haud yer han',' and ran with humped shoulders, lucky if his vast and expensive full-bottomed wig was not put out of action by a cataract of filth. The ordure thus sent down lay in the broad High Street and in the deep, well-like closes and wynds around it making the night air horrible, until early in the morning it was perfunctorily cleared away by the City Guard. Only on Sabbath morn it might not be touched, but lay there all day long, filling Scotland's capital with the savour of a mistaken piety.

G. M. Trevelyan, O.M. (*1876–1962*)
ENGLISH SOCIAL HISTORY: 'The Eighteenth Century'

Perhaps the first civic father to provide some sort of relief to his citizens was the Roman Emperor Vespasian (A.D. 9–79) who built a number of handsome urinals (gentlemen only). The chronicler tells us that he 'of his princely bounty and magnificence erected diverse places of fair polished marble, for this special purpose, requiring and no less straightly charging all persons, as well citizens as strangers, to refrain from all other places, saving these specially appointed'.

Making the use of the urinals compulsory gives a clue that Vespasian's action was not wholy benevolent. In true Roman style he also made a handsome profit by collecting the effluent in tanks and selling it to dyers.

Suetonius tells us that Vespasian's son Titus complained that the urinals and their tanks smelt. To which the father replied '*sed non olet denarius*'. 'But the money doesn't smell'.

133

Madrid is reported to have instituted portable privies on the back of carts. These toured the streets, heralded by a crier (what would he have cried?).

Even in Edinburgh there is record of an entrepreneur trying to provide some sort of relief:

> The streets of Edinburgh were perambulated by a man carrying a bucket and a great cloak, with the cry 'Wha wants me for a bawbee?' meaning 'Who wishes to hire the services of my bucket and shielding cloak for a halfpenny?'
>
> Lawrence Wright
> CLEAN AND DECENT

What the town-dwellers of the western world badly needed was the device that we now have; a hygienic container, washed with running water, with a valve system so that the effluent is borne away, odour-free, through a ventilated pipe.

Surprisingly, such devices have popped up throughout history. When Sir Arthur Evans excavated King Midas's Palace of Knossos in Minoan Crete he found it elaborately plumbed with a latrine complete with marble pan (which probably had a wooden seat) and a removable plug with a cistern of water above it to flush it clean. (It is said that when Sir Arthur was asked by somebody what the clay thing was which he was holding in his hand, he replied 'Tis an ill-favoured thing, sir, but Minoan'). King Midas's Palace was dated as about 2,000 years B.C.

In Elizabethan times a tremendous leap forward was made by Sir John Harington, Queen Elizabeth's godson. In 1596 he published a book which he called *Metamorphosis of Ajax* (in reference books the title is followed by the note – A pun on 'A jakes' – as inevitably as any reference to the writer 'Saki' is followed by – H. H. Munro).

In the book the author describes, and gives the plans of, a water closet which he has invented:

To. M.E.S., Esquire.
Sir,

My master having expressly commanded me to finish a strange discourse that he had written to you, called the Metamorpho-sis of Ajax, by setting certain pictures thereto... Wherefore now, seriously and in good sadness, to instruct you and all gentlemen of worship, how to reform all unsavoury places, whether they be caused by privies or sinks, or such like (for the annoyance coming all of like causes, the remedies need not be much unlike) this shall you do.

AN ANATOMY.

In the privy that annoys you, first cause a cistern, containing a barrel, or upward, to be placed either in the room or above it, from whence the water may, by a small pipe of lead of an inch be conveyed under the seat in the hinder part thereof (but quite out of sight); to which pipe you must have a cock or a washer, to yield water with some pretty strength when you would let it in.

If that which follows offend the reader, he may turn over a leaf or two, or but smell to his sweet gloves, and then the savour will never offend him. The cistern in the first plot is figured at the letter A; and so likewise in the second plot. The small pipe in the first plot at D, in the second E; but it ought to lie out of sight. The vessel is expressed in the first

Next make a vessel of an oval form, as broad at the bottom as at the top; two feet deep, one foot broad, sixteen

135

This is Don A JAX house, of the new fashion, all in sunder, that a workeman may see what he hath to do.

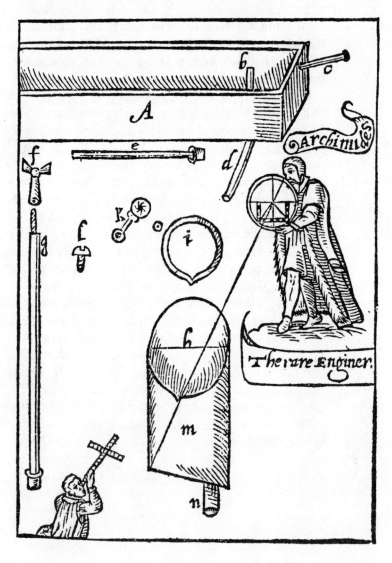

inches long; place this very close to
your seat, like the pot of a close-stool;
let the oval incline to the right hand.

*plot
H.M.N.,
in the
second H.K.*

This vessel may be brick, stone or
lead; but whatsoever it is, it should
have a current of three inches to the
back part of it (where a sluice of brass
must stand); the bottom and sides all
smooth, and dressed with pitch, rosin
and wax; which will keep it from
tainting with the urine.

*The current
is expressed
in the
second plot
K.
A special
note.*

In the lowest part of the vessel
which will be on the right hand, you
must fasten the sluice or washer of
brass, with solder or cement; the
concavity, or hollow thereof, must be
two inches and a half.

*In the
second plot,
I.L.*

To the washers stopple must be a
stem of iron as big as a curtain rod;
strong and even, and perpendicular,
with a strong screw at the top of it; to
which you must have a hollow key
with a worm to fit that screw.

*In the first
plot G.F.,
in the
second F.
and I.*

This screw must, when the sluice is
down, appear through the plank not
above a straw's breadth on the right
hand; and being duly placed, it will
stand about three or four inches wide
of the midst of the back of your seat.

*In the first
plot
between
G.I.*

Item, That children and busy folk
disorder it not, or open the sluice with
putting in their hands without a key,
you should have a little button or
scallop shell, to bind it down with a
vice pin, so as without the key it will
not be opened.

*This shows
in the first
plot K.L.,
in the
second G.;
such are in
the backside
of watches.*

These things thus placed, all about your vessel and elsewhere, must be passing close plastered with good lime and hair, that no air come up from the vault, but only at your sluice, which stands closed stopped; and it must be left, after it is voided, half a foot deep in clean water. *Else all is in vain.*

If water be plenty, the oftener it is used, and opened, the sweeter; but if it be scant, once a day is enough, for a need, though twenty persons should use it.

If the water will not run to your cistern, you may with a force of twenty shillings, and a pipe of eighteen pence the yard, force it from the lowest part of your house to the highest.

But now on the other side behold the Anatomy.

Here are the parts set down, with a rate of the prices; that a builder may guess what he hath to pay.

		s.	d.
A,	The Cistern: stone or brick. Price	6	8
b, d, e	the pipe that comes from the cistern with a stopple to the washer	3	6
c,	a waste pipe	1	0
f, g,	the item of the great stopple with a key to it	1	6
h,	the form of the upper brim of the vessel or stool pot		
m,	the stool pot of stone	8	0
n,	the great brass sluice, to which if three inches current to send it down a gallop into the JAX	10	0

Here is the same all put together, that the workeman
may see if it be well.

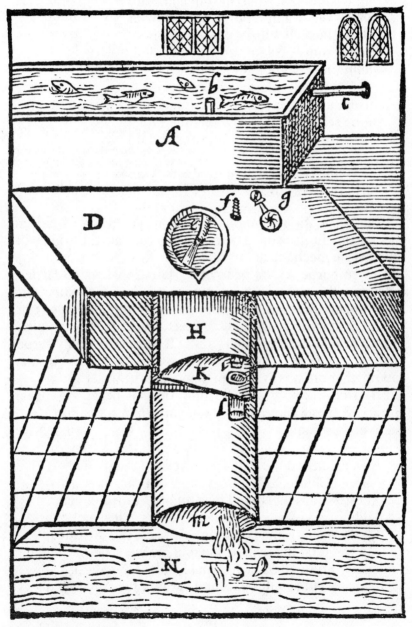

A. the Cesterne.
B. the little washer.   139

i,   the seat, with a peak devant for
           elbow room

The whole charge thirty shillings and eight pence: yet a mason of my masters was offered thirty pounds for the like.

... And this being well done, and orderly kept, your worst privy may be as sweet as your best chamber.

Sir John Harington (*1561–1612*)
A NEW DISCOURSE OF A STALE SUBJECT, CALLED
THE METAMORPHOSIS OF AJAX

> This specification embodies all the main features of the modern flushing valve-closet. One was constructed for Sir John on his estate at Kelston, near Bath, and another was installed in Queen Elizabeth's Richmond Palace, seemingly with some success.

What kept the invention away from the reach of citizens was partly the lack of interest in developing the somewhat crude valve mechanism but mainly the fact that water in cities had to be borne on the back of a professional water-carrier.

During the eighteenth century things began to stir again. Experiments were made to carry water from pumping engines along conduits to reach main streets, sometimes being piped into great houses to fill their tanks. It was usually only turned on for a few hours two or three days a week but it was cheaper, and much more was available, than from the water-man.

Fixed close-stools with flushing devices began to appear. Horace Walpole came across some in 1760, in the house of A Lady of Fashion:

> I breakfasted the day before yesterday at Ælia
> Lælia Chudleigh's ... Every favour she has
> bestowed is registered by a bit of Dresden china.
> There is a glass-case full of enamels, eggs, ambers,
> lapis lazuli, cameos, toothpick cases, and all kinds
> of trinkets, things that she told me were her
> playthings; another cupboard, full of the finest
> japan, and candlesticks and vases of rock crystal,

ready to be thrown down, in every corner. But of all curiosities, are the conveniences in every bedchamber: great mahogany projections, with brass handles, cocks, &c. I could not help saying, it was the loosest family I ever saw. Adieu!

Horace Walpole (*1717–1797*)
Letter to George Montagu, 27 March, 1760

Fifteen years later, and a hundred and seventy-nine years after Sir John Harington's *Metamorphosis of Ajax*, the first ever patent was taken out for a 'valve closet', an invention much along the lines laid down by Sir John. It did not work very well but in 1788 it was followed by another design patented by The Blessed Bramah. Joseph Bramah's design worked well and was the most popular model for the next hundred years. The 'water-closet' had arrived.

Enormously helped by the industrial developments of the nineteenth century, and spurred by dreadful outbreaks of cholera, the problems of bringing clean water to houses and taking dirty water away again were tackled, slowly but steadily. Glazed pottery pipes were invented to make hygienic sewerage disposal practical. Iron pipes were used for water-supplies in place of wood.

A sanitary engineer, George Jennings, agreed to provide hygienic latrines for visitors to the Great Exhibition in Hyde Park in return for being allowed to charge customers a small fee, thereby inventing the penny-in-the-slot public convenience (and the expression 'spend a penny').

Pottery manufacturers devised increasingly ambitious flushing systems:

Jennings' 'Pedestal Vase' won the Gold Medal
Award at the Health Exhibition of 1884, being
judged 'as perfect a sanitary closet as can be made'.
In a test, it completely cleared with a 2-gallon flush

10 apples averaging 1¼ ins. diameter
1 flat sponge about 4½ ins. diameter
Plumber's 'smudge' coated over the pan

141

4 pieces of paper adhering closely to the soiled
surface.

A simple test was that improvised by Mr. Shanks
who, when trying a new model, seized the cap
from the head of an attendant apprentice, thrust it
in, pulled the chain, saw it go and cried out
happily, 'It works!'

Lawrence Wright
CLEAN AND DECENT

By the 1900s there was a huge range of splendid 'water-closets' available, some intricately decorated, some clad in mahogany or disguised with a wickerwork seat but all with grand, dignified names.

Just as rural Americans tend to be nostalgic about the old privy in the backgarden, so urban Britishers tend to remember with emotion those fine old names like 'Belvedere' and 'Osborne'. It is one of the few aspects of last-century design that has not attracted the pen of Sir John Betjeman. However, Mr. Alan Bennett has stepped in on Sir John's behalf:

Bolding Vedas! Shanks New Nisa!
The trusty Lichfield swirls it down
To filter beds on Ruislip Marshes
From my lav in Kentish Town.

The Burlington! The Rochester!
Oh those names of childhood loos –
Nursie knocking at the door:
'Have you done your Number Twos?'

Lady typist – office party –
Golly! All that gassy beer!
Tripping home down Hendon Parkway
To her Improved Windermere.

Chelsea buns and lounge bar pasties
All washed down with Benskin's Pale
Purified and cleansed with charcoal
Fill the taps in Colindale.

Here I sit, alone and sixty,
Bald and fat and full of sin,
Cold the seat and loud the cistern
As I read the Harpic tin.

Alan Bennett (*1934–*)
PLACE-NAMES OF CHINA

The grandest of all baroque 'easences', the culmination of all advances in style and facilities since Sir John Harington's design, was built in Ulster to the wishes of a refugee from Hungary. Or so Spike Milligan tells us:

> The disintegration of the Austro-Hungarian Empire hit many people, especially those who had disintegrated with it. The Count Nuker-Frit-Kraphauser was one such notable. In the hiatus that followed the assassination of the Archduke Ferdinand, and the collapse of the Empire, he had fled his native Hungary in the jade of a revolutionary night with nothing save a small suitcase with three million pounds and some silly old crown jewels, but this fortune meant nothing; his greatest loss was having to leave the great majestic family Easence. The greatest toilet in the western world and the only consecrated one in the Holy Roman Empire.
>
> The Count Fritz Von Krappenhauser had fled to Northern Ireland, bought Callarry Castle, ten thousand acres, and a small packet of figs. For years he brooded over the loss of the ancestral abort. Finally worn out by indifferent, and severe, wood-seated Victorian commodes, he decided to build a replica of the family's lost masterpiece here in the heart of Ulster's rolling countryside. He employed the greatest baroque and Rococo architects and craftsmen of the day, and every day after; seven years of intense labour, and there it now stood, a great octagonal Easence. No ordinary

palace was this; from the early stone Easence of Bodiam Castle to the low silent suite at the Dorchester is a long strain, but nothing equalled this, its gold leaf and lapis lazuli settings gleaming in the morning sun, on the eight-sided walls great ikons of straining ancestors, a warning to the unfit. Through a Moorish arch of latticed stone, one entered the 'Throne Room'; above it, in Gothic capitals the family motto, 'Abort in Luxus'. From the centre rose a delicate gilded metal and pink alabaster commode. Six steps cut in black Cararra marble engraved with royal mottoes led up to the mighty Easence; it was a riot of carefully engraved figurines in the voluptuous Alexandrian style, depicting the history of the family with myriad complex designs and sectionalized stomachs in various stages of compression. The seat was covered in heavy wine damask velvet, the family coat of arms sewn petit-point around the rim in fine gold thread. Inside the pan were low relief sculptures of the family enemies, staring white-faced in expectation. Towering at the four corners, holding a silk tasselled replica of the Bernini canopy, were four royal beasts, their snarling jaws containing ashtrays and matches. Bolted to the throne were ivory straining bars carved with monkeys and cunningly set at convenient angles; around the base ran a small bubbling perfumed brook whose water welled from an ice-cool underground stream. Gushes of warm air passed up the trouser legs of the sitter, the pressure controlled by a gilt handle. By pedalling hard with two foot-levers the whole throne could be raised ten feet to allow the sitter a long drop; and even greater delight, the whole Easence was mounted on ball-bearings. A control valve shaped like the crown of Hungary would release steam power that would revolve the commode. There had been a time when the Count had aborted revolving at sixty miles an hour and been given a medal by the Pope.

White leather straps enabled him to secure himself firmly during the body-shaking horrors of constipation. Close at hand were three burnished hunting horns of varying lengths. Each one had a deep significant meaning. The small one when blown told the waiting household all was well, and the morning mission accomplished. The middle one of silver and brass was blown to signify that there might be a delay. The third one, a great Tibetan Hill Horn, was blown in dire emergency; it meant a failure and waiting retainers would rush to the relief of the Count, with trays of steaming fresh enemas ready to be plunged into action on their mission of mercy and relief. With the coming of the jet age the noble Count had added to the abort throne an ejector mechanism. Should there ever be need he could, whilst still in throes, pull a lever and be shot three hundred feet up to float gently down on a parachute. The stained glass windows when open looked out on to 500 acres of the finest grouse shooting moor in Ulster. He had once invited Winston Churchill to come and shoot from the sitting position. In reply Churchill sent a brief note, 'Sorry, I have business elsewhere that day.' From his commode, the Count could select any one of a number of fine fowling pieces and bring down his dinner. Alas, this caused his undoing. The boxes of 12-bore cartridges, though bought at the best shops in London, had sprung a powder leak. Carelessly flicking an early morning cigar, the hot ash had perforated the wad of a cartridge.

But to the day of the calamitous fire. It had been a fine morning that day in 1873. The Count had just received his early morning enema of soap suds and spice at body heat; crying 'Nitchevo!' he leapt from his couch. Colonic irrigation and enemas had made his exile one internal holiday. Clutching a month-old copy of *Der Tag*, and contracting his abdomen, he trod majestically towards his famed Imperial outdoor abort bar. A few moments later the waiting retainers heard a shattering roar and were deluged, among other things, with rubble.

'Himmel? Hermann? What did you put in the last enema?' queried the family doctor of the retainers.

Flames and debris showered the grounds and there, floating down on the parachute, came the Count. 'People will look to me when I die,' he had once said. His wish had come true.

Spike Milligan (1918–)
PUCKOON

An extraordinary aspect of this whole subject is that for something like four thousand years this place where every man and woman alive 'went' once or more every day has never, in any Western language, been given a simple, straightforward name.

A 'bath' was a 'bath' from the first, and one now visits the 'bathroom'. The hole in the ground, or the plank over the bucket, or the little shed have never been so honoured. Instead it has been referred to by a mass of coy, or poetic, or enigmatic euphemisms.

The Children of Israel went to 'The House of Honour'
The Ancient Egyptians went to 'The House of the Morning'
Monks went to the 'Garderobe' (our modern cloak-room'), or
The 'Necessarium' (later the 'Necessary House'), or
The 'Reredorter' (literally 'Room at the back of the Dormitory').
The Tudors went to the 'Privy' (A Place of Privacy), or
The Jakes (Jack's Place).
The seventeenth century added 'The Bog-House' (this

became a word much used by builders and was the technical term preferred by most architects until the early years of this century).

When one expression became too familiar, our more genteel ancestors found themselves a new one:

> Busy in painting some boarding in my Wall Garden
> which was put up to prevent people in the Kitchen
> seeing those who had occasion to go to Jericho.

The Reverend James Woodforde (*1740–1803*)
DIARY OF A COUNTRY PARSON: 26 April, 1780

'Jericho' was originally a slang word for a place of banishment or a hiding-place. 'Jerry' used as slang for a chamber-pot is supposed to have come from a different source, i.e. 'jereboam': a large bottle.

The above, and a great many more similar euphemisms for the same thing, refer only to the place itself, the room or hut or whatever, and not to its equipment, e.g. hole in the ground, or bucket with earth in it, or marble seat over conduit. Nor do they refer to its specific purpose.

When Mr. Bramah patented his so-called 'Valve Closet' (literally 'small room with a valve') and piped water arrived, and the beautifully made device began to be installed in more and more homes to make living sweeter, one might have thought that society would have found a name for It. But no. When a nineteenth-century citizen had converted a room into one of these new-fangled bathrooms, how did he describe the Thing to his friends? 'On the left I have the bath. And on the right I have the . . .' The what?

Unhappily the growth of technology coincided with the growth of the Victorian middle classes, who became the device's main customers. And the distaste for admitting that the body needed evacuation and there was a Thing upstairs for that purpose was so strong in much of Victorian society that the Thing never did get a name. Once more, as with the Place, the Thing was referred to by a hundred evasive words and phrases.

It is a legacy from which we still suffer. If an object has just one word to describe it there is no problem. A 'bath' is a bath. We know it to be a big thing which holds a lot of water and we can get in it and wash and sing a song and muck about a bit. The word 'bath' is not heretical, although the Christian Fathers denounced baths as inducers of sloth, vanity and evil thoughts. Nor is the word 'dirty' although ladies and gentlemen once used to bath together and do naughty things therein. Nor is the word 'vulgar and horrid' because one has to sit naked in a bath and clean dirt off one's salient features. The word for a bath is 'bath' and we all happily use it, unpunished by society.

It is a totally different matter with That Which Has No Name. We have got to use one of the euphemisms, and we have to choose the right one or we *will* be punished. Perhaps the last real barrier between Britain and the Classless Society is that each social class Goes to a different place.

The Aristocracy tends to go to the 'lavatory', the Middle Classes to the 'loo', and the Workers to the 'toilet'.

The picture, however, is constantly in a state of flux. There are indications that in the last few years there has been a strong – perhaps as high as 20% – swing towards 'toilet', which has taken over from 'bog-house' as the technical term adopted by architects, builders and municipal authorities. 'Loo' is holding strong and perhaps increasing its share of the market. It seems that most of the gains made by 'toilet' have been at the expense of 'lavatory'.

All three words are a mile away from describing a porcelain bowl with a seat on it. 'Lavatory' and 'toilet' are corruptions of useful words which described entirely different things: *The Shorter Oxford Dictionary* gives the original meaning of 'lavatory' as:

1. A vessel for washing, a laver, a bath.
2. The ritual washing of the celebrant's hands.
3. A lotion.

A 'toilet' was originally:

1. A piece of stuff used as a wrapper for clothes; a towel or cloth thrown over the shoulders during hairdressing.

2. A cloth cover for a dressing-table.
3. The articles required or used in dressing.
4. The table on which these articles are placed.
5. The action or process of dressing; the reception of visitors by a lady during the concluding stages of her toilet.

8c. Preparation for execution by guillotine.

Nobody is quite sure where the word 'loo' sprang from. One school of thought holds that 'loo' is a shortened form of 'Waterloo', a jocular corruption of 'water-closet'. Another holds that it is a throwback to the old Edinburgh shout of 'guardy-loo!' when a chamber-pot was about to be emptied out of a top window. However, it seems to date back in usage only as far as the late nineteenth century, which gives credence to a private claim that the original 'loo' was Lord Lichfield's aunt:

> The story of the origin of the word 'loo' was told me by the Duke of Buccleuch's aunt, Lady Constance Cairns. Your relations feature largely in it.
> In 1867 (Lady Constance was not absolutely certain of the date) when the 1st Duke of Abercorn was Viceroy of Ireland there was a large houseparty at Viceregal Lodge, and amongst the guests there was the Lord Lieutenant of County Roscommon, Mr. Edward King Tennison, and his wife Lady Louisa, daughter of the Earl of Lichfield.
> Lady Louisa was, it seems, not very lovable; and the two youngest Abercorn sons, Lord Frederick and Lord Ernest, took her namecard from her bedroom door and placed it on the door of the only W.C. in the guest wing. So in those select ducal circles everyone talked of going to Lady Louisa. Then people became more familiar – Jimmy Abercorn told me that when he was a boy one went to 'Lady Lou' (though he had never been told who Her Ladyship was).

149

Now in these democratic days the courtesy title
has been dropped, and within the last thirty years
or so – only really since the war – the term has
seeped down into middle-class and even working-
class usage. But it all really originates with your
Hamilton uncles being ungallant to your Anson
aunt; who I think should have her immortality
recognised.

The Hon. Sir Steven Runciman
Letter to Lord Lichfield, 11 June, 1973

Chances are that the word 'loo' probably drifted across the Channel into our language, as so many other words did.

The Continent must have as many euphemisms as we do: *le wattair* (short for 'the water-closet'), *le double* (short for 'the W.C.'). A widespread and curious form is using the number 100. One wild explanation of this is that it is an unsavoury pun on *la chambre cent* (room one hundred) and *la chambre sent* (room smelly). Be that as it may, many old Italian hotels label it *numero cento*, as do other regions, e.g., Cyprus. The theory is that the '100' became corrupted to 'loo'.

A faintly more plausible explanation is that 'loo' is an anglicised version of the French word *lieu*, or 'place'. On seventeenth century English architectural plans the 'loo' was often marked *le lieu*, and many signs in French 'loos' still read *On est prié de laisser ce LIEU aussi propre qu'on le trouve.* In Germany they use the same word, *der Locus*.

So as far as the origin of the word 'loo' is concerned, in the words of the old saying 'you pays your penny and you takes your choice'.

The difficulty with the three main euphemisms is that they are non-interchangeable. Those who go to the 'toilet' regard the use of the word 'lavatory' as disgusting. Those who go to the 'lavatory' find the word 'toilet' deeply depressing and vulgar. Goers to the 'loo' consider the word 'toilet' to be common and the word 'lavatory' to be revolting.

The social minefield becomes ever more complex when you consider that the three social classes themselves split into a number of sub-classes and society also splits vertically into sub-divisions like male and female, extrovert and introvert, urban and rural, bright and dim, each of which clings to its own euphemism and rejects the others as being in dreadfully poor taste.

When strangers meet and a thoughtful host wishes to offer the use of his privy to an unknown guest, or the guest urgently needs to locate it, each has to thumb his way mentally through a *mille-feuille* of potentially offensive expressions before choosing the one which, on the evidence of clothes, accent, bearing, conversational style, the other is most likely to consider 'correct'.

The range of expressions is vast. It includes:

For Use in Schools:
'Please may I be excused?'
'Please may I leave the room?' (a teacher reported that one of her charges once produced the sentence:
'Please, Miss, Johnny's left the room on the floor.')

The Approach Jocular:
'Just going to see whether the horse has kicked off its blanket'
'Where's the House of Lords, old son?'
'Must go and shake hands with an old friend'
'Just going to kiss the au pair goodnight'

The Approach Hearty:
'If you're busting it's the first door on the left'
'The bog's on the landing'

For Use in France:
'*Je veux changer le poisson d'eau*'

The Approach Coy:
'Anybody seek comforts?'
'I rather want potty'

151

The Approach Oblique (from hosts who find the subject embarrassing):
    'You've had a long car journey, would you like to . . . wash?'

The Approach Extremely Oblique (from hosts who are deeply embarrassed):
    'Would you like to go upstairs . . . or something?'

The Approach Almost Non-Existent (from hosts so miserably embarrassed that they cannot bear to say anything at all):
    (Vague, nervous hand movements are made, as though testing the weight of a pair of oranges)
    'Would you care to . . . ?'
    (The hand movements continue rhythmically until guest understands and answers. However long it takes).

Without a name it may be but the Thing now receives honour and attention because it is a household fixture on which money can be spent.

Powders in pastel colours are on sale to keep It clean and fresh.

Blocks of scented substances are available to dangle in Its vicinity so as to give the impression that It smells of flowers or citrus fruit or woodland pine.

Its seat may be soft and spongy to sit upon, or warmed by electric current.

Its lid can be made pretty with a fluffy bonnet.

And why, after all these centuries, should Its importance to our way of life *not* be recognised?

It is upon It, seated, that great books have been read, great ideas have been formulated; and will be again.

It is here, in peace and privacy, that our day begins:

>Seated after breakfast
>In this white-tiled cabin

Arabs call *the House where*
Everybody goes,
Even melancholics
Raise a cheer to Mrs.
Nature for the primal
Pleasures she bestows.

Sex is but a dream to
Seventy-and-over,
But a joy proposed until
　we start to shave:
Mouth-delight depends on
Virtue in the cook, but
This She guarantees from
Cradle unto grave.

Lifted off the potty,
Infants from their mothers
Hear their first impartial
Words of worldly praise:
Hence, to start the morning
With a satisfactory
Dump is a good omen
All our adult days.

Revelation came to
Luther in a privy
(Crosswords have been solved there):
Rodin was no fool
When he cast his Thinker,
Cogitating deeply,
Crouched in the position
Of a man at stool.

All the Arts derive from
This ur-act of making,
Private to the artist:
Makers' lives are spent

Striving in their chosen
Medium to produce a
De-narcissus-ized en-
   during excrement.

Freud did not invent the
Constipated miser:
Banks have letter boxes
Built in their façade,
Marked *For Night Deposits*,
Stocks are firm or liquid,
Currencies of nations
Either soft or hard.

Global Mother, keep our
Bowels of compassion
Open through our lifetime,
Purge our minds as well:
Grant us a kind ending,
Not a second childhood,
Petulant, weak-sphinctered,
In a cheap hotel.

Keep us in our station:
When we get pound-noteish,
When we seem about to
Take up Higher Thought,
Send us some deflating
Image like the pained ex-
   pression on a Major
Prophet taken short.

(Orthodoxy ought to
Bless our modern plumbing:
Swift and St. Augustine
Lived in centuries,
When a stench of sewage
Ever in the nostrils

Made a strong debating
Point for Manichees.)

Mind and Body run on
Different timetables:
Not until our morning
Visit here can we
Leave the dead concerns of
Yesterday behind us.
Face with all our courage
What is now to be.

W. H. Auden (*1907–1973*)
THE GEOGRAPHY OF THE HOUSE
(for Christopher Isherwood)

ACKNOWLEDGMENTS

Grateful thanks are due to the following authors, agents and publishers for permission to quote copyright material.

The Author's Literary Estate and Chatto and Windus Ltd for *The Young Visitors*, by Daisy Ashford. Faber and Faber Ltd and Randon House Inc. for 'Encomium Balnei' and 'The Geography of the House' from *Collected Poems* by W. H. Auden, edited by Mendelson. Alan Bennett for permission to print, for the first time, the complete text of his poem 'Place-Names of China'. To John Murray Ltd for 'Business Girls' by John Betjeman. Creativity Ltd, A. P. Watt Ltd and Harold Ober Associates Incorporated for *Imperial Women* by Pearl S. Buck, Copyright © 1956 by Pearl S. Buck. William Heinemann Ltd and Mrs. James L. Clifford for *Dictionary Johnson* by James L. Clifford. Dobson Books Ltd for *Nanny Says: as recalled by Sir Hugh Casson and Joyce Grenfell*. Victor Gollancz Ltd and the Estate of the late A. J. Cronin for *The Stars Look Down* by A. J. Cronin. Faber and Faber Ltd and E. P. Dutton and Co. Inc. for *Prospero's Cell* by Lawrence Durrell. Hutchinson Publishing Group for *The Collected Ewart 1933–1980*, © Gavin Ewart, 1980. The Estate of Michael Flanders, and Donald Swann, for 'In the Bath' and 'The Spider' from *The Songs of Michael Flanders and Donald Swann*. A. D. Peters and Co. Ltd for 'The Bedchamber Mystery', by C. S. Forester. Martin Higham for *A Book of Anecdotes* by T. F. Higham MA. Diana Holman-Hunt for *My Grandmothers and I* by Diana Holman-Hunt. McIntosh and Otis for a poem by Edward Newman Horn. Martin Secker and Warburg Ltd for 'Lines to a Bishop who was shocked (A.D. 1950) at seeing a pier-glass in a bathroom', from *A La Carte* by Sir Lawrence Jones; and for *Aubrey's Brief Lives* edited by Oliver Lawson-Dick. Sir Steven Runciman for permission to print his private letter to the Rt. Hon. the Earl of Lichfield. Spike Milligan for *Puckoon*, published by Michael Joseph and Co. Methuen London, the Canadian publishers McClelland and Stewart Ltd of Toronto and E. P. Dutton and Co. Inc. for 'Vespers' by A. A. Milne from *When We were Very Young*, Copyright, 1924, by E. P. Dutton and Co. Inc. Renewal, 1952, by A. A. Milne. Jonathan Cape Ltd for 'Adrian Mitchell's Famous Weak Bladder Blues' from *Out Loud* by Adrian Mitchell. April Young Ltd for The Glums episode by Frank Muir and Denis Norden. Curtis Brown Ltd on behalf of the Estate of Ogden Nash, and Little, Brown and Co., for 'Samson Agonistes' from *Verses from 1929 On* by Ogden Nash: copyright 1942 by The Curtis Publishing Company; first appeared in *The Saturday Evening Post*. Hamish Hamilton Ltd for *Historical Memoirs* by Duc de Saint-Simon: translated by Lucy Norton. The Estate of the late Sonia Brownell Orwell, Martin Secker and Warburg Ltd, and Harcourt Brace Jovanovitch Inc. for *Such, Such Were the Joys* by George Orwell. William Heinemann Ltd and the author for *Delights* by J. B. Priestley. Faber and Faber Ltd, and W. W. Norton and Company Inc., for *A Cambridge Childhood* by Gwen Raverat. The Specialist Publishing Co. in California for *The Specialist* by Charles Sale. Penguin Books Ltd for *The Cottage Garden* by Anne

157

INDEX